SPEECH
THERAPY

SPEECH THERAPY

65 PICK-ME-UPS TO GET YOU THROUGH
MANY OF LIFE'S WHAT-THE-F*CKS

The Captain

~ Now with ~
More Words,
More Wisdom,
~ and Even ~
More WTFs

HARPERONE
An Imprint of HarperCollinsPublishers

ORIGINALLY PUBLISHED AS *SPEECH THERAPY* IN THE UNITED STATES OF AMERICA IN 2021 BY THE AUTHOR.

FIRST HARPERONE HARDCOVER PUBLISHED 2025.

Designed by Yvonne Chan

Illustrations by Travis Gray

Library of Congress Cataloging-in-Publication Data has been applied for.

ISBN 978-0-06-341405-1

25 26 27 28 29 LBC 5 4 3 2 1

Disclaimer: This is <u>not</u> a *how-to* book;
this is a *help-your-mood* book.

Enjoy the following pages.
Even when life feels unenjoyable.

For Ashley, even though she continues to ignore my advice.

And for everyone who's ever experienced something
in life that made them say,
What the fuck? Why is this happening to me?

CONTENTS

Chapter 1: Down in the Dumps After Being Dumped 1

Chapter 2: Buyer's Remorse 3

Chapter 3: Money Misery 6

Chapter 4: A Furry Companion Destroys a Possession 8

Chapter 5: Laid Off, Fired, and Lacking Desire 10

Chapter 6: You're Not Perfect (and Nobody Else Is Either) 13

Chapter 7: Somebody Cheated (and It Wasn't You) 15

Chapter 8: Butting Heads 17

Chapter 9: Your Favorite Plant Took a Dirt Nap 20

Chapter 10: Damn It, You've Been Locked Down (Again) 22

Chapter 11: Horrible Horoscope(s) 24

Chapter 12: You Failed, Now What? 27

Chapter 13: Car Trouble 29

Chapter 14: Stranded on a Desert Island 31

Chapter 15: Co-Parenting Conundrums 33

Chapter 16: Homeowner Hell 36

Chapter 17: HOA Horseshit 39

Chapter 18: Dealing with a Bad Roommate 41

Chapter 19: Your House Is Literally on Fire 43

Chapter 20: Endlessly Embarrassed 45

Chapter 21: Caught in a Compromising Situation 47

Chapter 22: The Death of a Pet 49

Chapter 23: You Have the Right to Remain Silent 51

Chapter 24: Your Team Lost 54

Chapter 25: You've Been Catfished 56

Chapter 26: Ruined Your Favorite Outfit 59

Chapter 27: A "Special Date" Mistake 61

Chapter 28: FOMO: Focus On Moving On 63

Chapter 29: You've Been "Cancelled" 65

Chapter 30: Woke Up on the Wrong Side of the Bed 67

Chapter 31: You've Hit a Creative Wall 69

Chapter 32: Lost Luggage While Traveling 72

Chapter 33: You've Been Rejected. 74

Chapter 34: You're Sick AF. 76

Chapter 35: Woke Up with a Hangover 78

Chapter 36: You've Lost Your Shit 80

Chapter 37: Online Arguments and Accusations. 82

Chapter 38: You've Been Robbed. 84

Chapter 39: Stuck in a Rut 86

Chapter 40: Fell for a Financial Scam 89

Chapter 41: Bitten by a Rattlesnake 91

Chapter 42: Regret Parting Ways 93

Chapter 43: You've Let Yourself Go 95

Chapter 44: Leaked Nudes or a Sex Tape. 97

Chapter 45: Credit Fraud 100

Chapter 46: Outnumbered or Unsupported 102

Chapter 47: Sorry, Wrong Person 104

Chapter 48: Triggered. 106

Chapter 49: Kink in Your Neck. 108

Chapter 50: Bamboozled by Somebody 110

Chapter 51: So, You're Going to Be a Dad. 112

Chapter 52: When Court Is Your Only Option 114

Chapter 53: Missed Your Shot 117

Chapter 54: You're Late 119

Chapter 55: Stepped in Dog Shit 121

Chapter 56: A Sore Loser and a Sore Thumb. 123

Chapter 57: Got an STD (Maybe?) 125

Chapter 58: Somebody Ate Your Leftovers. 127

Chapter 59: When You Gotta Go, You Gotta 130

Chapter 60: BFF Backstabbing 132

Chapter 61: Just Can't Catch a Break. 134

Chapter 62: Abducted by Aliens. 136

Chapter 63: Disastrous Dating. 138

Chapter 64: Bugged Before Bedtime 140

Chapter 65: Your Boat Has a Hole in It 142

1

DOWN IN THE DUMPS AFTER BEING DUMPED

Damn, it's over . . . now what?

Whether you're the breaker or the breakee, the end of a relationship is never easy. However, getting dumped is undoubtedly the less desirable of the two roles, so let's focus on that for the remainder of this little heartbreak chat.

Let's be honest, getting dumped fucking sucks. I've been there, your friends have been there, and pretty much every human on Earth over the age of thirty has been there as well. In other words, your heartbreak is nothing special. Now, as harsh as that sounds, the lack of originality is actually a good thing. Because although it might seem like you're currently alone, suffering from something that nobody else can understand—let alone relate to—you're wrong. Billions of people have gone through exactly what you're going through. And guess what? They got through it. In fact, the majority of them will probably tell you they're a stronger person, not in spite of it, but rather, because of it.

There is quite literally only one way to get through what you're currently going through and that is to simply allow yourself to go through it. If you're hurting, it means you're on the path to healing. In life and love, you must feel whatever it is that you want to heal. Ignoring your pain, pretending you aren't heartbroken, or distracting yourself with somebody else isn't going to help you process the breakup. You might be able to fool yourself (and others) for a moment, but an unhealed past is a setup for a future crash. Friends, family, and random dudes writing books can help you feel better, but nobody else can do the work that will truly make you better. You have to do that shit yourself, and it all starts by sitting with yourself. Seriously, stew in your emotions like you're soaking in a hot tub of heartbreak until you acclimate to what has happened. Once you've done this, you're ready to process.

Acknowledge the relationship—all of it—the good, the bad, and the ugly (emotionally or physically). Permit yourself to feel gratitude for what the relationship meant to you and what the relationship can, or already did, teach you. What did you learn? How can you take this personal growth and apply it to a subsequent relationship? What did you discover about your likes, your dislikes, and your nonnegotiables? What did you like most about yourself in the relationship?

Where did you potentially lose yourself? There's a lot to analyze, and even more to internalize. This will take time, but with effective use of that time, you will be better than fine, just like the billions of other humans who have been heartbroken before you. Lastly, if you're worried you don't have the strength to move on, think of just how much strength you are using to hold on—then, redirect that energy and enjoy your life. And your next relationship.

2

BUYER'S REMORSE

Just because *money doesn't grow on trees* doesn't mean it can't be burned just as easily. And, during the times when your bank account feels like a wildfire has just come through and wiped it out due to unbridled spending, it can be hard to think about anything else. Especially if you recently made one of those life-changing purchases like a new car or a house. So, when your initial rejoice becomes immediate remorse—what do you do?

First of all, I get it. I've been there. I bought my first house then subsequently fell into my worst financial year of a decade. It almost broke me; and believe me, I regretted buying that damn house every day for nearly a year while struggling to get my bills paid. But the one thought that brought me comfort was reminding myself who I was when I decided to buy it. I didn't know what the future had in store for me financially; I was truly buying the house because I wanted a large yard for my son, my family, my dogs, and farm animals that were yet to come—why would I beat myself up over that? My intentions were to provide a homestead, not to purchase an extravagant home for my own ego.

Likewise, you can't beat yourself up for buying something that you genuinely desired at the time and had the financial means of making a reality. When you made the decision, you were a different person (a past version of yourself); you didn't know what you know now, and you didn't have the information that you now hold. So, rather than guilt-trip yourself, remind yourself of your intentions and understanding at the time.

I've also personally found that the root cause of nearly all moments of monetary regret stem from my obsession of *not being wrong*. I hate making the wrong decision, I hate feeling taken advantage of, and I really hate feeling dumb or irresponsible. More often than not, it's my fanatic fear of "being wrong" that inevitably becomes "buyer's remorse." The thought that haunted me the most about buying my first house was thinking that I bought during the "wrong time," when the markets were high, mortgage rates weren't optimal, and waiting may have saved me a lot of monetary misery.

But here's the truth of both my situation and yours: If you can't return it, there's literally no benefit in regretting it. You have to accept your decision; remember *why* you made it in the first place—and if you still regret it in a few days, a few weeks, or even a few months, learn from your financial fuckup in order to be wiser with your finances in the future. Don't allow yourself to be pressured, guilted, or manipulated into a lifestyle or purchase that truly doesn't fit your budget. Other than that, enjoy what you have. Take pride in the fact that you were in a position to make such a purchase— *seriously, congratulations, you've earned it (literally).*

On another note, regardless of whether you've made a healthy purchase or an irresponsible mistake, if your buyer's remorse has put you in a dire financial situation, turn to the next chapter, entitled "Money Misery," and let's start problem solving.

3

MONEY MISERY

Surprises are great. Birthday parties, vacations, and nights spent in the bedroom are always better with a surprise or two (three if you're feeling kinky)—but surprises of the financial kind aren't always enjoyable. I mean, unless you just won something, surprises that involve money are stressful.

Nobody wants to be surprised by an unexpected bill or a sudden loss of income; nothing in life brings out our anxiety, or burdens us with worry, quite like money. And, if there's one thing I know for certain about money, it will always be surprising us (good and bad). Money both comes and goes as quickly as the wind blows. Whether it's a layoff, a hospital bill, or the rapid collapse of a stock that once seemed so promising, the worry of not knowing how you'll pay for something can be downright crippling. As somebody who received the dreaded *your insurance does not cover this* response after the birth of my son, I know damn well the sleepless nights and stress-blurred days that come from wondering, *How the fuck am I going to pay for this?* And another thing that I know damn well is this: Stress, frustration, and self-pity has never helped me pay for anything. In fact, allowing myself to be overcome by these "feels" has only ever made the situation more costly of an ordeal. It's manifestation in motion.

In the field of psychology, our tendency to dwell on the illogical downside of something is known as *catastrophizing*—a cognitive distortion that causes us to jump to the absolute worst possible conclusion—which we do far too often when it comes to our finances. It's an unfortunate inclination to have because every second that you spend worrying on the worst of it is a second that you could spend working through it—devising a plan, a strategy, a budget, or an inventive idea to get you out of your monetary hole.

When facing a financial obstacle, you have to remove the mental obstacles that are preventing you from thinking rationally or creatively. Stress clouds your focus, playing the blame game blurs your head with bullshit, and thinking with a catastrophic mentality will have you believing, *There's no way I'm going to recover from this.* A clear head is at the core of all problem solving; it's what allows you to think proactively instead of problematically. There's always a plan if you're open to finding it, and that plan just might, well . . . surprise you.

4

A FURRY COMPANION
DESTROYS A POSSESSION

It almost feels like betrayal, doesn't it? I mean, you welcomed this child—whether furry or of the human variety—into your home; you feed them, care for them, perhaps even dress them, and what do you get in return? A shit-stain on the new rug, tooth marks in your favorite pair of heels, and a pile of broken glass adjacent to the table where your expensive lamp used to rest. You respond by relegating your pet or child to an inferior position in the household for a while. *Go to your room!* or *Get in your crate!* you shout with haste, but is that really what you want? Nah. What you really want is a sense of control, and you gain a little control when you control where your child or animal must go. (It's also a valid form of punishment that can prevent the act from happening again, but I'm not here to discuss parenting styles with you—to each their own; I'm simply here to help you cool down after a cat-, dog-, kid-, or llama-related meltdown.)

Here's the deal: When we welcome a child or an animal into our lives, we relinquish a bit of control. That's the implicit trade that humans have been making for millennia. And this is precisely one of the reasons why I believe having pets or children is so beneficial for our humanity. When we exchange independence, freedom, and cleanliness for companionship, purpose, and the reward of caring for something outside of ourselves, we gain a new perspective. A perspective that is worth more than any material possession (yes, even your new Louboutins are worth less than your mind-set). Why else would humans continue having children and pets despite their inevitable destruction? Well, because they're worth it. The experience of genuine connection is far more enjoyable than any possession. And very few things will illustrate to you the *importance hierarchy* in your life as quickly as watching a new puppy tear through your closet. Fortunately, just as quickly as an item can be destroyed, an animal or child can fill your life with joy. Don't let the negativity of a chewed sneaker or a carpet stain cloud you from seeing all the positive things that your life has gained.

Now, I get it, I like nice shit just as much as the next guy or gal—but having nothing in your life to care about or connect with doesn't make your life more glamorous or independent; in fact, it typically means you're uptight and inflexible, aka "anal." Having pets or children can make you a better person simply because it teaches you to be more easygoing, understanding, and accepting of life's unexpected (not always desired) outcomes. A life that's too clean, too manicured, or too planned is not a life that I personally believe is worth living. A life without mess is a life without purpose (feel free to quote me on that).

5

LAID OFF, FIRED, AND LACKING DESIRE

Of all the bad hands to be dealt in life, being fired or laid off tends to be near the top (right behind death, severe injury, or imprisonment). Now, unless this is one of those rare occurrences when losing your job is actually a relief—maybe you intentionally got fired because you hated your boss, your co-workers sucked, or the job itself was too much of a mindfuck—losing your job can, and likely will, deliver a significant blow to your self-esteem. Not to mention, potentially delivering a hit to nearly every other aspect of your life, such as your housing, your sense of security, your relationship, etc.—but, you've probably already thought about all of that, so let's move on instead of reinforcing that fear and uncertainty. I want to help you discover a solution to keep swimming instead of towing you back under the thoughts that have you drowning.

In my life, I've had many different jobs: car wash attendant, warehouse worker, security guard, repo man, and more. Believe me, I know what it's like to be in between jobs because I've been there many times myself. And there are no other words to accurately define it: It's fucking hard. At one point in time, I spent a solid two years looking for a full-time job. It's stressful, frustrating, and personally defeating. I know exactly how you feel, but I also know that dwelling on those feelings is not going to change your situation. The best thing you can do, starting today, is build momentum. And you build this momentum however you can, not just with things that are work-related—you build it in all areas of your life, every day, and in every possible way.

Focus on improving your life in whatever aspects are within your control; doing so will make the uncontrollable shit feel a hell of a lot more bearable. Work on your fitness, your personal growth, your mental sharpness, or your relationships (or help another human being with any of those things). Go for a run, read a book, learn to meditate, spend some quality time with your partner. Any area of your life that has room for development, identify it and make the decision to improve it. The momentum that you build will naturally spill into your job search; you will benefit from increased confidence, more energy, less stress, and a better sense of purpose in your own life, and the purpose that you have in the lives of others. Whatever you do, don't let this period of finding employment for yourself become a period of feeling sorry for yourself. Do whatever it is that you need to do to maintain your daily momentum—and protect it; create a routine and stick to it. And, with time, you'll be back to the grind. I mean, hopefully you find a job that doesn't feel that way, but hey, at least you're back to getting paid, right?

NOTE: There's a good chance that improving the nonwork-related areas of your life will shift your outlook in a way that leads to you beginning to look for entirely different types of work. And, because I can't think of anything insanely clever right now, let's call it a "refocus bonus," and it's something that you never would have received had you remained stuck in your old ways.

6

YOU'RE NOT PERFECT
(AND NOBODY ELSE IS EITHER)

If you ask me, one of the most detrimental things that we, as humans, do to ourselves is believe that other people aren't humans themselves. We idolize those we see on social media, on streaming platforms, and in limited social settings, holding them to standards or ideals that are simply not rooted in everyday reality. And the things that we idolize the most about them become the very things that serve as our basis for comparison: appearance, wealth, talent, status, etc. We fall for the illusion of their perfection—instead of remembering the fact that we're all disgustingly human. We nitpick ourselves to death and imagine others are nitpicking us with the same judgmental ferocity. This is why something as insignificant as a zit, as temporary as a bad hair day, or as normal as a birth mark can literally fuck up our entire mind-set. The gist: When we compare ourselves, we nitpick ourselves. And, when we nitpick ourselves, we believe others are nitpicking us too. Meaning, we turn things as little as a pimple into a big fucking deal because we falsely believe others will as well. We create problems where there are none, which is exactly what happens when you pick at a zit that you should have just left alone.

In the field of psychology, this is known as the *spotlight effect*: a predisposition for the overestimation of what people are actually noticing about us or how many people are simply noticing us at all. In other words, when we're hyperfocused on something we don't like about ourselves, we tend to believe everybody else is hyperfocused on it too, which is typically not the case at all. (Trust me, your zit is not taking the center stage in any play other than your own.)

How many times have you allowed the spotlight effect to put you on voluntary house arrest, opting to stay inside rather than risk being seen in any state other than your "best"? Seriously, take a moment to think about this. How many good times have you missed out on, or how many good times did you fail to fully embrace, because you were overly concerned about something as trivial as a blemish? Is that any way to live? The answer is, most assuredly, *NO*.

So, what happens when you stop believing in the illusion of perfection? Well, the spotlight goes out and you stop judging yourself for the shit that makes you human. There are no gods or goddesses walking among us and nobody is immune to feeling self-conscious. Self-confidence is a choice. And it's a choice that only you can make. Now, put down this book and go enjoy your date—you look fucking great.

7

SOMEBODY CHEATED (AND IT WASN'T YOU)

I wanted this to be a separate topic from the breakup chapter of this book because cheating is especially painful, and potentially life-changing. The cutting discovery of infidelity can leave scars for years, or even decades, beyond the initial wounding. A singular occurrence in life can become a lifetime of self-doubt, suspicion, and fear. You might be asking yourself, *What did I do wrong?* And, more often than not, the answer to that is: absolutely nothing. Cheating says everything about the other person—their desires, their feelings, perhaps the shit in their own life that needs healing—and quite honestly, nothing about you. So, before you spend too much time raking yourself over the coals trying to figure out why your companion decided to touch somebody else's boobs or balls, you have to understand that although it's personally painful, infidelity is not always personal.

First things first, cheating is the fucking worst. Why? Because we're humans, and unlike our furry friends in the animal kingdom, sex for us is an emotional investment. In other words, it's normal to feel like shit because you're not a fucking rabbit. For most of us, being cheated on feels like being stabbed in the heart. And, chances are, you might feel like stabbing something (or somebody) right about now. However, as both a writer and someone who once seriously considered becoming a lawyer, you should probably restrain from doing anything that could result in you becoming an inmate—believe me, I don't know you, but orange is not your color.

If somebody cheats on you, rather than focusing on retaliation, focus on self-preservation. Do whatever it is that you need to do to keep it together and continue moving forward. For some, that means asking questions in order to fully understand what in the hell just happened. For others, it means leaving the room and never looking back. Just as every relationship has its own complexities, everyone will have their own list of healing necessities. Now, however you choose to move on, don't forget that closure can only come from one person: yourself. Don't rely on the individual who just betrayed you to now be the one who will emotionally save you. Closure is a gift that you give yourself, not a present that you wait to receive from somebody else. To gain closure, you might want answers, but you don't need them—what you really need is time and a focused mind.

Right now, focus on yourself. Focus on your actions, focus on your feelings, and focus on who you want to be as a person. Don't allow cheating to negatively change you. Sure, it might take a while before you're ready to open up and trust someone again, and that's fine, so long as you remember this: Cheating is not the end of the line when it comes to finding the love of your life. Lastly, if somebody doesn't choose you, let them fucking lose you. Once somebody has made up their mind, have the self-respect to stop wasting your own time.

8

BUTTING HEADS

In life, you must do what's right for you; you must make the move that you believe is the right move. Even if that means your words or decisions are the catalyst of a fight. Because disagreements are usually brief, but the resentment that comes from self-betrayal doesn't easily leave. So, even though a blowout with a partner, a friend, or a family member might have you feeling all hot and bothered, rest assured, if you spoke what you deemed to be true—or acted in support of the truth— you did the right thing. And I will back you up on that premise each and every time (so long as that "truth" is rooted in facts and not the temporary feelings associated with personal attacks). *Seriously, if somebody is truly upset with you for being honest, have them email me for clarification: TheCaptain @itsnoneofmyfuckingbusiness.com.*

Now, speaking of truth, there are two truths in every relationship—be it romantic or platonic: 1) You will have disagreements. 2) You will have compromises. However, fear of the first should never be the reason for the latter.

Don't compromise just because you're afraid of confrontation. If you don't speak your mind, that's not a compromise, that's a cover-up. And what you're covering up is your true self. A lifetime spent censoring yourself is a lifetime spent living for somebody else. Here's the cool thing about being honest with yourself and others: Most fights can be avoided altogether. Agreeing to and/or setting false expectations because you are afraid of a disagreement will truthfully lead to far more disagreements than honesty ever will. Even the little fights that seem to come out of nowhere are typically rooted in an underlying, long-held resentment that has been building after years or months of repeated self-censorship and unwarranted compromise.

Now, let's say that both of you have spoken your truth—or at least what you believe to be true—and you're proud of yourself for doing so, but the fight continues late into the night (your poor neighbors). This is not uncommon; we're talking about two humans with completely different life experiences and expectations. How do you reach a state of compromise in this situation? Well, you remove the need to be right. Because as soon as you remove the need to be right, you open yourself up to the possibility of being wrong, which puts you in a place to potentially learn something. But, what if you know you're right? Like, I mean, you FUCKING KNOW IT. What then?

Well, that's when you go back and reread the first paragraph. That's when your desire for honesty must outweigh whatever pain or negativity might be coming your way. By no means does it mean you should fight with your ego until the other individual agrees; quite the opposite, it means you should strive to be humble yet confident enough to argue without an emotional wall or ulterior motive.

In life, your ego is what feeds the need to be right. And, when you truly know you're right, there's actually no need to prove it. Speaking from your heart won't always be heard by others, but as long as you said or did exactly what you believe you needed to say or do in order to remain true to yourself, that should be all the proof you need. After that, it's time to let empathy, priority, and maturity decide whether or not there's a compromise worth making.

9

YOUR FAVORITE PLANT TOOK A DIRT NAP

Ah, a real Philodendron conundrum, or perhaps a *Monstera deliciosa* disaster—maybe just a Ficus *fuckup*? Whatever it is, it sucks. (You should know I had to Google every one of those plant names.)

Now, a lot of people might find it odd to be upset over the death of a houseplant—I mean, *It's just a plant*, right? Not to you. That plant was a representation of caring for something outside of yourself. And, chances are, it's not so much the loss of the plant itself that's painful, but the loss of time and energy that's really getting to you. The time that you put into caring for your plant, the time that you spent growing accustomed to seeing your plant and associating it with your definition of "home," and obviously the time that it took for your plant to grow. The real loss here is time. And, whether it's a houseplant or a failed relationship, feeling like we've lost time (or worse, wasted it) is something that, consequently, takes time to process.

I know people who have had the same plant for ten years or more. At that point, that plant becomes more than just another possession. It's living proof that your care and attention can lead to the growth and creation of something with beauty and longevity (again, similar to a relationship). So, if you ask me, being bummed about the death of a long-term chlorophyll companion is completely understandable. The good news: You don't have to bury a dead plant because it's already in the dirt.

Personally, I've never grown attached to houseplants, so even though I can't directly relate, I can still empathize with the loss of something that took a lot of time and consistency to bring to life. And, as inconsequential as the earlier statement was, it truly is just a plant, which is a good thing because that means you can replace it. You obviously can't replace your time or your money—large, mature houseplants can be surprisingly expensive—so I believe the best view to take here is this: Like most things in life, the joy of houseplants comes from the process of watching them grow. And starting that process by bringing home a new potted roommate is an opportunity to experience that all over again. (However, if you're looking for a roommate that's low-maintenance and a hell of a lot cuddlier than a cactus, might I suggest a cat.)

10

DAMN IT, YOU'VE BEEN LOCKED DOWN (AGAIN)

Now, you know I couldn't write this book without addressing the hell that was 2020. The year that fucked with all of us—but, since you're reading this, it means you made it through it. All of it. The financial, emotional, physical, mental, spiritual, political, and scientific confusion of a year that will go down in history. What if it happens again? For all our sakes, pray to whatever face in the sky you believe in that it doesn't. But, what if it does? Well, read on and I'll tell you what I'm doing, and perhaps, what you can do as well.

First, I'm learning from my mistake, and next time, I'm trusting my gut from the get-go. When it comes to any kind of large, life-changing situation—be it a worldwide quarantine, a career shift, or a relationship that doesn't feel right—trusting your gut is a surefire way to save your future self the regret that comes from second-guessing. From the beginning, my gut told me that quarantine was going to be much longer than two weeks. I didn't want to believe it. I got way too comfortable with the idea of doing absolutely nothing while I "waited it out," treating it like a mandatory vacation from the stress and frustrations of everyday life. So, if I'm ever "locked down" again, or sent to prison, I'm immediately settling in for the long haul (after thoroughly taking action to avoid the situation, of course). If my gut tells me this is something that is going to take a while, well, you better believe I'm going to find something to do that will make the entire ordeal worthwhile.

I'm also going to avoid the reverb chamber of social media. Because whether it's quarantine or a painful breakup, whenever you're going through something difficult, I strongly believe the best thing that you can do—not just for your survival, but for your sanity as well—is disconnect from external drama as much as possible. Now, I'm not saying you should bury your head in the sand and pretend whatever's happening isn't happening, but I am absolutely saying the following equation is accurate in this type of situation:

Too Much Alone Time + Social Media = A Distorted Reality

Keep that equation in mind any time you're dealing with something that can be easily influenced by outside opinion. Because nothing will make a breakup harder to deal with than seeing the lives of others looking "so damn perfect," and nothing will make being stuck in your home without a job more challenging than seeing others out living the life that's currently unavailable to you. When shit hits the fan, the greatest thing you can do for yourself is focus on improving yourself or the world around you, without the inundation of opinions, tide of negative emotions, and theater that is social media.

11

HORRIBLE HOROSCOPE(S)

We need to talk.
—The Universe

Few things will strike fear into your heart quite like the aforementioned four words. Whether it's your boss, your best friend, or your baby mama—when somebody says, *We need to talk*, that talk is probably not going to be a light-hearted or fun conversation. More often than not, the talk is going to revolve around something that needs to be addressed, corrected, or smashed altogether. But what about when the conversation feels like it's coming directly from the Universe? Like a Taurus in a china shop, what do you do when it feels like the Universe is about to wreck you?

Now, I've never been someone who puts too much weight into horoscopes, zodiacs, astrology, tarot, or whatever else—but I'm also not going to be someone who dismisses those beliefs if they truly help you make sense of your life. Why? Because life is fucking hard and confusing; we all need something that helps us find direction. For some, that direction comes from religion, politics, or science. For others, it's crystals, stars, and cards. The way I see it, whatever works for you, works for me (as long as you don't force it on me). Anything that encourages you to seek positive outcomes, new opportunities, or beneficial change is worth believing in. However, the truth with any religion, political affiliation, or spiritual connection is that they often use sweeping, vague generalizations that can feel oddly personal due to what's known as the *Barnam effect*, or the *Forer effect*. This is our psychological human tendency to interpret broad or impersonal traits as coming from within us or being connected to us. This is why false prophets can fool a congregation, experienced psychics can guess their way through a reading, and horoscopes can appear scarily accurate—whether good or bad, true or false, applied or assumed.

But no matter what you believe, I believe you will always find what you're looking for. For example, if I tell you that after reading this page you are going to meet a stranger within the next seven days who will have the power to completely change your life—and you decide to believe me for whatever reason—you will carry that thought in the back of your mind as you encounter each and every new person over the coming week; you will treat them differently, perhaps you will talk a while longer, act a little kinder, and think to yourself, *Is this*

THE person? All because you are looking to fulfill that idea of a stranger changing your life. And, well, you might even find someone who does just that because you were hyperaware and looking for it. I believe horoscopes and astrology work in this way because they encourage you to think about something that might not have been on the forefront of your mind until you read something to trigger it. They can then become self-fulfilling prophecies because you are actively seeking their fulfillment.

So, if you believe something bad is going to happen to you just because you read it in your cards this morning, well, chances are, something bad will happen because you are expecting it—you will find something bad just to prove it. But, if you don't want it to be, don't give that fear and negativity any of your energy. Similarly, if you believe something good will happen, you will find something good. You are the creator of your destiny.

12

YOU FAILED, NOW WHAT?

If you're reading this, you've failed (or will fail in the future). Failing is just as much a part of life as breathing. Without oxygen, you'll die. And, if you allow a failure to keep you from trying again, you might as well be dead—because what's the point of living if you're going to quit so easily?

Plain and simple, failure fucking hurts. And, despite the optimistic opening paragraph, I know I dwell on my own failures far longer than I should (something that I'm actively working on). But, as someone who has taken a lot of risks and failed probably just as often as I've won—both professionally and personally—I can tell you with absolute certainty that everything I said in the first paragraph is an unequivocal truth. If you have any hopes of getting what you desire out of life, you must view failure as a teacher. I may not be the quickest student, but I am a student, nonetheless—and I'm always willing to retake the test.

Failure is a vital part of history. Nearly every individual who ever did something notable with their life did not do so in spite of failure, they did so because of failure. Failure drives innovation and forces us to find a better way to do something. You've probably heard the following quote attributed to Thomas Edison (however, knowing what I know about the man's reputation,

I have my doubts as to whether or not he actually said this himself or "borrowed" it from somebody else): "I have not failed. I've just found 10,000 ways that won't work."

Now, regardless of who originated it, that is a great fucking quote. And that mind-set will pretty much guarantee success to anyone who applies it. While quotes like these can serve as motivators, what really matters in terms of overcoming failure is your character. Motivation is short lived and can easily be shaken, but character can last forever. Motivation is simply a feeling, whereas character is what's created when a collection of all your failures, your attitude toward them, and your willingness to keep going are combined into an unstoppable force. To put it comparatively, motivation helps with a quick gain, but character plays the long game. And the long game will always provide for those who are willing to play it. Like a seasoned card counter at a Blackjack table, every time you lose a hand (i.e., "fail"), you can put that information to use when playing the next hand, and the next, and the next . . . giving every failure a future purpose.

13

CAR TROUBLE

Assuming you're an adult who pays their own bills (or at least tries to), there's no sound more disheartening than the sputter, hiss, or whine of a car that's not going to get you to where you need to be on time—or at all. Whether it's the TV remote, a smartphone, or a car's engine, when technology or mechanics fail to work, it's hard to not have an immediate reaction that makes the situation worse. Our reactions can easily become more of an inconvenience than the actual inconvenience that's causing us to react in the first place. So, when something as substantial as a vehicle lets you down, how can you handle it instead of the situation handling you?

Let's be honest, cars kind of suck, or at least our reliance upon them being reliable does. Not many things have advanced society quite like the invention of the automobile; subsequently, not many cities have an infrastructure that isn't dependent upon owning a vehicle or at least having access to one—via ridesharing, a generous family member, or a friend with vehicular benefits. I'm not saying there aren't plenty of ways to get around without a car, I'm just saying, car trouble is especially frustrating when you're accustomed to always driving.

The stress of car repairs can go from zero to one hundred on the scale of "Overwhelming Shit to Deal With" in mere seconds.

And, like all major mishaps that you'll encounter on the road of life, the only way to keep your mind from running off the road is to pull over and allow yourself time to think things over. Essentially, you must break down your breakdown: 1) What's your immediate replacement or mode of transportation? 2) What's your long-term plan to get around? 3) What the fuck is actually wrong with your car? 4) Can you fix it yourself or do you need someone else? 5) How will you pay for the parts for the repair? 6) Is this repair even worth it or is your money better invested in a newer, more reliable vehicle? These are all important questions and considerations, but not all of them need to be answered or figured out immediately. Address them one at a time so you can still focus on the rest of your life.

Now, if you ask any survival expert the key to staying alive when you're stranded in the wilderness, every single one of them will say something along the lines of, *Stay calm and have a plan that focuses on the most important things first.* Don't overwhelm yourself. And, well, surviving without a car for a few days to a few weeks can feel just as dire and isolating as being stranded on a desert island (which is the exact situation that I'll get into in the next chapter).

P.S. Breaking down your breakdown works in a hell of a lot more scenarios than just a car that won't start. Whether it is mechanical or mental, breakdowns happen to us all—but we can always get back on the road by taking the time to analyze what happened, then repairing what needs repairing.

14

STRANDED ON A DESERT ISLAND

Damn, that's a lot of water . . . and sand. Fortunately for you, you've miraculously washed ashore with this book in hand, which should help you maintain a positive outlook (or, at the very least, you can burn these pages for warmth after reading).

Now, it probably goes without saying, I've never personally been stranded on an island. If I had, you would have definitely heard about it because I probably wouldn't shut up about it. However, I have spent a lot of time outdoors. I grew up hunting, hiking, and camping all over the great state of Utah; I also worked at a survival school for a month or so when I was nineteen years old. And the one thing I do know for certain about any survival situation—and pretty much every other life occurrence that tests your ability to survive hard times—is this: Your attitude really does make all the difference.

The thoughts you carry, the decisions you make or don't make, and the emotions that you either control or succumb to will quite literally make or break you. So, if you're going to be stranded with yourself on an island for God knows how long, be somebody who you would like to be stranded with.

Think about this: If you're stranded on an island with someone, you don't want to be stranded with someone who's pessimistic, hopeless, or unimaginative. You want to be stranded with someone who's level-headed, innovative, and determined. And, well, since you can't always count on others—neither on this island nor back home—you must be that person for yourself. Be someone who genuinely believes they will survive. Because the commonality among every survivor, from prisoners of war to lost hikers and forgotten sailors, is the belief that they will survive. If they didn't believe it, they wouldn't have done everything within their power to survive it.

In life, when we're put in circumstances that require us to rely solely on ourselves, we must master our mind. When we can't control our environment, we have to control our view of that environment. That's not to say that there won't be times when it feels like all hope is lost, but when those times do come, you'll have what it takes to not be overcome by those thoughts.

Now that we've addressed the importance of your mental state, you'll need to secure three things posthaste if you want any chance of getting off this island: water, shelter, and food. In that order. Good luck.

15

CO-PARENTING CONUNDRUMS

I started this book with a chapter about breakups, ending with the advice of *redirecting your energy in order to move on*— however, there are times when moving on isn't really an option. If you share a child, that's just not possible. You can *move forward*, but you can't just move on entirely. (I mean, you can, but only if you're okay with being a missing mom or a deadbeat dad.) The reality is, when kids are involved, breaking up isn't as simple as taking back your toaster, your favorite hoodie, and your DVD collection. Co-parenting requires you to evolve your relationship rather than erase it. *(But seriously, why do you still have all of those DVDs anyway? You're clearly clinging to the past in more ways than one.)*

Now, if you're reading this book, I imagine you are someone who likes to figure things out—something that both you and I have in common. And, if you're reading this particular chapter, you're in a co-parenting situation, yet another thing we share. In my personal experience, co-parenting is a lot like riding a bike, except you and the bike have a history together because you went for a ride at one point that created a child, and going for another ride now is only going to complicate an already complex situation. So, whatever you do, don't get back on the bike unless you're planning to buy it this time around. But definitely treat co-parenting like riding a tandem bicycle in the sense that you will need to find balance and work together if you want to move forward. Sure, you might not always be pedaling at the same time or at the same speed, but you are equally important to your child's future, which will require you to have a shared direction.

Some of the best advice that I received about navigating my own co-parenting situation is to treat it like a business relationship. I like this advice because that's essentially what it is now: You're in the business of raising children. So, just like you wouldn't be late to a meeting with your boss, or you wouldn't talk about inappropriate things with your co-worker—or sleep with your co-worker because it can cloud your judgment and thinking— you should strive for the same level of professionalism with your ex. Focus on the task of raising your kid(s). You aren't required to talk about anything other than that, unless friendship is something that both of you have decided to pursue. Personally, I believe if you can be friends, it's better for everyone. But I know not everyone can do that.

Now, as with any job, you have to discuss boundaries, budgets, and timelines, and most importantly, you have to *communicate* these decisions and desires with one another. Talk, text, call,

email—*hell, buy some walkie-talkies if you have to*—it doesn't matter how you do it, just do it. Similar to how a business will fail if two partners are running it with opposite strategies, your child doesn't stand much of a chance if his or her parents are working against each other. So, talk, and talk often.

Lastly, I know co-parenting can be hard and emotionally heavy. And, at times, you just want to quit, move to Bali, and go all *Eat Pray Love* on your shit, but that's not realistic—unless your ex also agrees to it, and you decide to do it together *as a family.* After all, you are still a family—just a different type of family— and family should always come first. As long as your kids know that they are a priority in your life, they're going to be fine. And you're going to be fine as well . . . even though it might not feel like it right now.

16

HOMEOWNER HELL

There's always something . . . and if you own a home, condo, or even a timeshare, you know this all too well. Owning your own place can sometimes feel like throwing your money into a furnace (which needs a tune-up before winter by the way) instead of feeling like the independent dream that was sold to you by society. Sure, you don't have a landlord anymore, but do you know what you have instead? Termites. And termite treatment is thousands of dollars.

Here's the deal: The moment any home is built, Mother Nature wants to take it down. And, if you don't stay ahead of her attempts—which she will send at you in the form or rain, snow, wind, winged wood-eaters, and tectonic shifts—you can bet your ass that she will eventually win. Why? Because no home is built to last forever, just like nobody is going to live forever. So, until we figure out the immortality of the human race, there will likewise always be something in your home that needs to be fixed, updated, or replaced. There are three guarantees in life: death, taxes, and home repairs.

But, if you're smart about it (and lucky enough to evade natural disasters), your home will last long enough for you to sell it to somebody else, allowing your problems to become their problems, and your memories to become the foundation of their memories—while you sail off into the sunset with (hopefully) some equity and a nice return on your investment.

I know the stress of keeping up with maintenance of a house can take both the fun (and the funds) out of having your own place—believe me, I've felt it myself—but there's one thing that has helped me remain positive and take pride in my decision to buy. And that is: playing the long game. Because it's damn near impossible to lose any game when it's played long enough. There's a great quote by Michael Jordan that says, *I've never lost a game; I just ran out of time.* The same is true with real estate; with enough time, you can't really make a bad investment. Just take care of it until it's time to sell it.

Similar to your body (the home of your soul), if you take care of it, you can live in relatively good function as you get old. And if you put work into your relationship, you can enjoy that old age with somebody by your side. The point I'm trying to make here is this: If you take care of something, that something will often take care of you—be it your house, your body, or your spouse. But that doesn't mean it won't occasionally be hard. Eating healthy gets boring, home repairs are fucking annoying, and putting in the work to make your relationship work can sometimes definitely feel like, well, work. But there's a lot of pride to be found in taking care of something, whether it's your body, your relationship, or a nice three-bedroom with no HOA (we'll talk about that nightmare next).

Now, as important as it is to take good care of your investments, it's still fun to let loose from time to time and treat your body like a house party full of stolen liquor. Just make sure that you fix anything that breaks before it becomes a bigger problem.

17

HOA HORSESHIT.

Ugh, three-letter agencies . . . the FBI, the CIA, the NSA, the IRS—and the most corrupt and controlling of them all—the HOA. Seriously, nothing says the three words, *We hate fun,* quite like a three-letter agency led by a bored old woman named Susan.

I mean, it's one thing to have the government spy on you through your cellphone, but it's an entirely different thing to have a nosy neighbor tracking your every move, peeking over the hedges, and reporting you to the board because you painted your front door *juniper* instead of *sage*. *Are you fucking serious, Susan?! It's still GREEN!*

Now, whether it's a spouse, a friend, a parent, or the motherfucking HOA president, how do you deal with others telling you what to do? Personally, I don't think there's anything more frustrating than somebody else telling you how to live, where to live, or what color to paint your own fucking door. And if you go through life trying to fight with everyone who disagrees with you, you're going to be exhausted and miserable. Whether on the battlefield or in your neighborhood, picking your battles is absolutely necessary for long-term success and sanity. If you turn everything into a fight, you're going to be fighting your entire life.

So, if the HOA wants you to repaint your door to the approved color, just repaint your damn door. Honestly, you shouldn't have moved into an HOA-restricted area in the first place if you weren't willing to play by the rules. That's like voluntarily entering a state prison then getting upset about the lack of breakfast options. But, I get it, even though you chose to move into an HOA, it's still annoying to be told what to do all the time. So, in that case, it's time to employ another military tactic: the tactic of the double-agent. *If you can't beat 'em, join 'em.* Infiltrate the HOA and put some of your own rules in place; dismantle Susan's regime from the inside.

The truth is, as you go through life, there will always be someone with an opinion on how you're living—that's unavoidable. HOA or not, there will always be someone who wants to tell you which color to paint your door. And, with social media, these opinions are more prevalent than ever, which is why you need to be more diligent than ever when it comes to analyzing your decisions before you make them. Take the time to really think about what you're doing to ensure that it is what YOU actually want to do, and not what you feel like you have to do because of group opinion. And, if you're someone who likes to make their own decisions and prefers their independence without outside influence, both HOAs and social media comment sections are a death sentence. Avoid each of these like Susan avoids having sex with her husband.

18

DEALING WITH A BAD ROOMMATE

Are you living with a human or a hamster? Because I've seen rodents keep their cage cleaner than your condo.

Okay, maybe your roommate isn't a slob. Maybe you have a completely different set of issues with your current housing companion. Regardless of what those issues are, your home is supposed to be a place for you to escape from the outside world; it's a place to recharge and be yourself—and a bad roommate can make your sanctuary feel like a prison. But, what can you do? Moving is a pain in the ass and your name is on the lease too. Well, it's time to suck it up and be honest. Have a straightforward talk with them, and if the situation can't be resolved, it's probably time one of you found a new place to live. However, you'd be surprised how many situations can be fixed with a simple conversation. Quite often, it's our feelings of resentment toward a person that make conditions seem more unbearable than they really are. The majority of people want to be a good roommate and believe they are—hell, maybe it's you that could be better? (You'll never know unless you're willing to talk like two adults.) Quick story: I once had roommates (yes, plural) who would use the paper towels when we ran out of toilet paper. And, well, since you can't flush paper towels, they would just put them in the trash.

Now, I know moving sucks (trust me, I moved six times, across the country and between states, in five years), but avoiding your home—or hiding when you're there—is far worse than the inconvenience of relocation. The toll that comes from not having a proper place to unwind, reflect, and prepare for each day will weigh you down in all areas of your life. In fact, I can't tell you how many people I've known who have seen their depression and anxiety completely dissipate by simply finding a new roommate (or getting their own place altogether). If you're familiar with gardening, you know that sometimes all a plant needs to come back to life—and truly grow—is new soil. What if I told you that changing your living situation can have the same dramatic effect? The energy that you derive from an environment (and the people in it) will determine how you feel, the goals you pursue, and the decisions that you make on a day-to-day basis. Living with someone whose energy repels your own is an indirect form of self-betrayal. Not to mention, life is simply too damn short to spend it splitting the rent with someone you don't even like sharing your time with.

Your space needs to be a place where you can be you; a place where you can do what you need to do to keep doing whatever it is that you do, day in and day out. And, although it might seem like a financial burden or too much of an inconvenience at this time, I guarantee you that the emotional expense of living with someone you don't vibe with will cost you more in the long run.

19

YOUR HOUSE IS LITERALLY ON FIRE

Okay, I'll admit, a house fire is something that I've spent far too much time thinking about. So much time that I've already selected my go-to fire outfit in case I ever have to rush out of my house in the middle of the night. Why have I done this? Because I want to look good if I'm interviewed on the local news while my house smolders in the background. You know, with an outfit that says, *I don't know what's hotter, my house or this sweet robe?*

Now, in all seriousness, so long as my family, pets, and houseguests escape safely, I do believe I could emotionally recover from the loss of a property quite quickly. Maybe it has something to do with how often I tend to move, maybe it's something that comes with age, or maybe it's the universe trying to remind me of what's truly important in life. Whatever the reasoning, I just don't have a strong attachment to "things." I mean, I still enjoy nice shit, but I don't need nice shit. That's not to say that I wouldn't be upset to see everything I own go up in smoke, but I do believe I'm in a place now to recover from it better than ever—due to a conscious understanding of my attachment to objects.

By no means am I undercutting how fucking traumatic a natural disaster can be, particularly when your livelihood is uprooted in such a way that even the necessities become scarcities. I hope you never experience it, but if you do, when it comes to your possessions, recognizing the psychological construct known as *object attachment* is a valuable tool to have in your recovery arsenal. Object attachment is the emotional experience we have, either good or bad, when we hold, see, or think about a particular object in our lives. It is the literal emotion that we attach to it. Maybe it's love, security, or happiness. This is why we don't feel as confident when we leave the house without our favorite jacket, or why we feel a sense of loss after parting ways with a piece of furniture that's been in the family for generations. Unless there's a utilitarian purpose to owning it, it's not the item itself that you miss; it's the memory or feeling that you've associated with it.

We like how "our stuff" makes us feel. So, when we say an item is "irreplaceable," what we're really saying is, *Nothing else makes me feel the way that this particular item makes me feel.* And, although that may be true, it's never wise to attach too strongly to something that can be taken from you. If you ask me, memories are the only things that are truly irreplaceable. As long as you have those, you can weather any storm or tragedy.

20

ENDLESSLY EMBARRASSED

Why did I do that? Why did I wear that? Why did I say that? Ah, the dreaded self-talk that comes along with anything that impacts your self-esteem. It's not fun, and it's certainly not productive.

Maybe you bombed an important speech, maybe you looked dumb trying something new, or maybe you just made a decision that turned out to be the completely wrong one. Whatever you did, or did not do, I can tell you this: Your feelings of embarrassment are entirely your own doing.

Who decides what's embarrassing and what's acceptable anyway? Your friends? Nope. Your colleagues? Nah. Society? Not really; the majority of people are so busy with their own shit that they don't even care what you're doing to begin with. So, who decides what's embarrassing and what's not? Well, you do. It's completely your choice. Something that embarrasses you probably won't embarrass me, and vice versa. Granted, it doesn't feel like much of a personal choice when you're dealing with the remarks, comments, and laughter of individuals who are trying to make you feel like you have no say in the matter. Learn to laugh at yourself and you won't even hear the laughter of somebody else.

Growing up, I allowed embarrassment to control my life. If I did something wrong, or something that I believed made me look "dumb"—just once—that was usually enough for me to never try again. And, looking back, I'm bummed to think about just how many experiences I missed out on because I was overly concerned about looking uncool or feeling embarrassed. I was already expecting situations to go wrong before even trying. And one of the most wrong things that you can do in life is allow the fear of embarrassment to control your life. You will miss out far more than you will avoid messing up.

Now, let's redefine what it means to do something "embarrassing." Instead of embarrassing, let's call it what it really is: something unexpected, different, unique, or simply out of the norm that society has agreed upon. When you think of it this way, who wouldn't want to do something embarrassing? Hell, doing embarrassing shit sounds fun. Doing something unexpected is exciting. Doing something different is motivating. Doing something unique is powerful. And when you choose to redefine what's deemed embarrassing into something that's simply contradictory to other people's behavior, you become empowered. Even if others laugh or make snide comments, they will secretly wish they had your confidence. They will say things like, *Aren't you embarrassed? . . . I'd be SO embarrassed.* And your response will be, *Honestly, I couldn't care less.*

21

CAUGHT IN A COMPROMISING SITUATION

Your personal time is meant to be just that: personal. So, what happens when your time alone is seen by somebody else in your home? Maybe a roommate, a sibling, or, worst of all, a parent.

Don't act like you aren't already thinking about exactly what I'm talking about: getting caught in *flagrante delicto* with yourself— that's a fancy Latin phrase I use for masturbating so I hope you treated yourself to a nice dinner first. In simpler terms, somebody walked in on you with one hand down your pants and your other hand . . . well, I don't really need to (or even want to) know what it was doing. Because regardless of your hand positioning or the creativity of your imagination, I'm pretty sure I know exactly what you're currently feeling: shame.

Ah, shame, a most vile and wretched human emotion. Has shame ever done anything good for anyone? In some situations, maybe. For the sake of playing devil's advocate, if feeling shame causes you to change your behavior in a way that later benefits yourself or society, I guess shame could be deemed beneficial. However, when it comes to playing with your privates, shame promotes the kind of self-loathing and sexual suppression that can ultimately lead to a lifetime of unhealthy behaviors and potentially violent acts toward yourself or others.

Nothing will make you feel dumber, more embarrassed, or more remorseful than shame-induced turmoil. The self-shame spiral can go deep, and it can last for fucking weeks; in some cases, your entire life. And, from my personal experience—not with getting caught masturbating, because I've always been smart enough to double-check the lock, but with many other things in my life that have caused me to feel shameful about my actions—the best way to get rid of it is to fucking own it. Shame is like a cancer: It grows with time. You know, like that dirty family secret that nobody wants to talk about for so long that it eventually becomes a formidable family legend. Believe me, the last thing you want is for your little self-induced incident to become something more significant due to prolonged silence. When we choose to talk about things, especially the shit that's awkward or embarrassing, we take back our power in the situation. And it doesn't have to be much; you don't have to have a lengthy conversation about what you were doing, all you need to do is literally break the silence. Make a joke, acknowledge the awkwardness, ask if you can borrow a Kleenex.

I mean, unless you were pleasuring yourself to something extremely fucking weird or taboo—like a cup of Ramen noodles or a *National Geographic* article about global warming—all

you need to do is clear the air in order to clear the shame from the room. Again, you have nothing to be ashamed of, a little self-love never hurt anybody. If anyone should be ashamed, it's the person who walked in on you without knocking. Where are their manners before entering? What, are they a fucking cop or something?

22

THE DEATH OF A PET

Ah shit, if you're going through this, I'm sorry to hear it. I've been there and I know it hurts.

With the death of my first dog, I was a slobbering mess; I left the vet's office with more snot, tears, and drool on my face than someone who just lost one of those Fourth of July hotdog eating contests. At the time of my dog's death, I'd been fortunate enough in my life to not have lost any friends or close family members; putting down my dog was my first real experience with loss. And, in my opinion, the hardest thing about losing a pet is losing that part of our lives that was completely untarnished. Our relationships with our pets differ from any other relationship because we don't have anything to prove to them, we don't have to change ourselves to be accepted by them, and the relationship itself is based purely on companionship—there are no goals outside of simply enjoying time together. In this way, our pets allow us to be our most authentic selves. They make us better because they show us who we are when we're not guarded, fake, or concerned with our reputation. Pets make us pure and honest. I mean, if you can't be honest with your dog, who can you be honest with?

I once had a conversation with a friend the night that she lost her dog. In this conversation she said, *He was the best part of me,* to which I promptly replied, *No, he wasn't. He just allowed you to be the best version of yourself.* This conclusion is not something that I would have ever truly grasped had I not gotten another dog six years after the passing of my first. When I brought my new puppy home, it only took a few weeks to once again understand and truly experience the unique relationship between animal and human: a relationship without expectation or personal gain, a relationship that's simply all trust, all the time. This puppy taught me what I had forgotten about, and he helped me, once again, open those closed-off parts of myself. Plain and simple, dogs and other pets—yes, even cats (I have one sitting on my lap as I write this)—make us better if we choose to embrace the relationship. Who we are with our pets is who we should strive to be with other individuals: trustworthy, reliable, and real.

The loss of a beloved pet is indeed a time for mourning, but it's also a time for gratitude—a time to say, *Thank you.* Be grateful for everything that animal taught you about living. And, if you truly want to honor them, don't be an asshole to other people for no reason. Be like a dog and learn to accept others despite their flaws. . . . Seriously, do you have any idea how many things your dog had to ignore about you?

23

YOU HAVE THE RIGHT TO REMAIN SILENT

Well shit, if you're reading this, your mind must be running faster than your legs did the night you were arrested—or else you wouldn't even be in this situation, right? *I mean, damn, the last time you were in handcuffs at least there was a ball gag involved.*

Okay, jokes aside, we all fuck up. Some of us more than others, some of us in ways worse than others, and some of us in ways that others would find simply unimaginable. I'm not here to judge (the one in the courtroom will be doing that), I'm only here to write from one human to another.

First of all, this is not the end. Sure, it might be the end of many things, but it is not the end of everything—serving time is not the end of your life, nor your contribution to this world. Rather, this is a beginning. The beginning of something that has the power to reshape the remainder of your life, and it's now up to you to determine what shape that new life of yours becomes. There's a fantastic quote about this by Viktor Frankl, a Holocaust camp survivor and pioneer of *logotherapy* (purpose-driven psychology): *When we are no longer able to change a situation, we are challenged to change ourselves.*

This is what going to jail or prison is: a challenge to change yourself. Your physical freedom can be taken from you in many ways, but your freedom to change can never be stolen or inhibited. So, whether you're looking down the barrel of a nickel or a dime, the mental challenge of serving time is going to be the most challenging aspect of your impending incarceration. But you can succeed in overcoming that challenge by finding purpose in a daily routine; in doing so, you will find the person you are able to become.

Now, if you can create a routine that positively affects each of these three areas of your life, you'll be setting yourself up to deal with whatever lockup has in store for you. 1) Physical: Take care of yourself as much as you can. Because when your body is healthy, it's easier for your mind to be as well. 2) Mentally: Read, write, create, discuss, and learn—the better your mind, the better your time. 3) Spiritually: Whether it's religion, meditation, or group therapy, a lot of purpose comes from acknowledging something, or someone, outside of yourself.

As for the specifics of what you're about to face, well, I don't know anything about your case, your state, or your history, but I do have several friends that have served time for a variety of crimes, and they have all told me that having a routine and creating a purpose (especially being useful to others) is what saved them—so, good luck. Lastly, I highly recommend finding a way to get your hands on a copy of Viktor Frankl's book *Man's Search for Meaning*. In my opinion, it will be much more helpful to you—and what you're about to go through—than this book; although, I do hope this short passage has provided some perspective.

P.S. Don't eat the oatmeal. I don't know why, but someone told me that once.

24

YOUR TEAM LOST

First, let's talk about identity. A quick Google search for "identity" gives us this definition: the fact of being who or what a person or thing is.

Or, to put it simply, your identity is you. It's who you are at your core, who you are without any titles, objects, or affiliations. Your identity is the amalgamation of the characteristics that make you who you are: your beliefs, your personality, your sense of humor, etc. And, as we grow older and learn to interact with our environment in search of stimuli, reassurance, and security, we begin to attach our identity to a variety of external things: our job, our social status, our possessions, or a specific team that we believe represents us.

Now, attachment is normal. Throughout our lives, we all do it. Because we're all humans and that's just what humans do: We attach to things that bring us pleasure, understanding, or a sense of belonging. After all, isn't everything more exciting when you feel like you have some skin in the game? Of course it is; that's why sports betting is the easiest way to up the intensity of whatever's happening on the court or on the field. However, when our identity becomes directly linked to an external outcome, it's no longer just a game; we're quite literally playing with our emotional well-being.

For years, I was attached to a job that I held in New York City. And it wasn't until I quit that job that I realized that role really wasn't me; it was an attachment that controlled my way of thinking. Once I released that, I was able to get my life back on track.

So, if your team losing is enough to derail you entirely, you're having a crisis of identity. And, as with any addiction or unhealthy attachment, the first step toward overcoming it is admitting it. No team should be your reason for living, or the reason your night is completely ruined. It's fun to be a fan of competition, but goddamn, if a loss leaves you feeling like you, yourself, are a loser—even if only temporarily—you're not living for yourself; you're living vicariously through the accomplishments and failures of somebody else.

25

YOU'VE BEEN CATFISHED

There's a complex array of feelings that comes from being catfished as opposed to just being led on in the traditional sense. This is because it's difficult to put your finger on what was real and what was entirely fake, which can make moving on harder than other forms of deceit. After you've been catfished, you'll have trust issues, your self-confidence will be crushed, and you'll feel dumb as fuck.

"Why me?"

"Why would somebody do that?"

"How could I have been so stupid?"

These questions are likely going to go unanswered, which means you'll have to make peace with yourself and what happened without the closure that most people desire at the end of a relationship. And, like any relationship—yes, catfishing can still be considered a relationship (albeit a unique one) because your feelings were still real even though they were totally being fucked with—creating your own closure is the best way to regain your self-confidence.

Here's the thing: Hope is a powerful human emotion, perhaps even the most powerful human emotion. There's nothing else quite like it; hope carries with it endless potential. Unfortunately, that potential is sometimes the potential to be easily deceived. Catfishing relies on hope, and those that catfish others might even have some hope of their own, helping them justify their selfish, duplicitous actions. The lesson here is not to remove hope from your life, because living in hopelessness is a horrible existence; rather, the lesson here is to realize that you weren't dumb, you were hopeful. Sure, you might have made some dumb decisions, but you made those decisions out of an abundance of hope—not because you're a dumbass.

In life, hope can make you just as strong as it can make you vulnerable. You can and should have hope about things that matter to you, but you can't allow hope to influence you in a way that causes you to disregard obvious conflicts. This is true in all aspects of life—catfishing, business, politics, real-world relationships, etc. If hope blinds you to the obvious, you're playing a game that's very high risk. In the early days of social media, people weren't as wise to the warning signs of being led on by someone who wasn't who they were representing themselves to be. Social media was a frenzy of friending, commenting, and engaging with strangers that you otherwise would have no means of meeting in your daily life (that remains the upside of social media and dating apps: an expanded social circle). A lot of people have been catfished without even knowing it. You're certainly not the only person this has happened to, and you definitely won't be the last (trust me, the metaverse is going to get real fucking weird).

Being catfished totally fucking sucks, especially when your feelings were very fucking real. But nothing sucks as bad as letting it affect you in a way that doesn't allow you to heal. Throw that ugly-ass fish and the negative feelings about yourself back in the water, then go meet a real stranger in the real world. It's far more rewarding than social media will ever be—have some hope.

26

RUINED YOUR FAVORITE OUTFIT

There are a number of reasons why a particular article of clothing becomes your go-to for going out. Most likely, it's for one of these two reasons though: It's either incredibly fucking comfortable or makes you feel super-fucking confident.
For those reasons, a stain, a tear, or a devastating washing machine occurrence can make for a depressing morning, afternoon, or evening. (Don't even get me started on family heirlooms or meaningful hand-me-downs; we already covered that in the house fire chapter of this book.)

Now, as the saying goes, *The jacket doesn't make the man or woman; the man or woman makes the jacket.* You can replace the word "jacket" in that sentence, and it will remain just as accurate. It doesn't matter what it is—a shirt, a pair of pants, a bra, etc.—all that matters is that whoever is wearing it has made the decision to fucking own it. (This is why celebrities can get away with wearing outfits that most people wouldn't dare leave the house in.) So, even though your favorite sweater or T-shirt might be ruined, there's no reason for your confidence to unravel right along with it. I'm not saying you shouldn't be dismayed; after all, clothes cost money and finding something that fits your body perfectly isn't always easy. What I'm saying is, you might be bummed, but with the right attitude your days of looking fly are far from done.

At the time that I'm writing this, I currently own a black denim jacket that's probably the best jacket I've ever owned. It's easily my favorite piece of clothing and it's become my go-to whenever I step outside after sundown. It fits perfectly, the color is ideally faded, and I can make it work for pretty much any occasion (I've actually never washed it for fear that any of that might change). I'd definitely be a little down if something were to happen to it. But, at the same time, it might also be a good thing because I know I wear it too much. It would force me to mix things up and try something new. And what fun is life or fashion without some innovation?

If you ask me, the only thing that feels better than putting on your favorite piece of clothing is putting on a new piece of clothing that makes you feel absolutely fucking great—finding a new favorite. This sartorial debacle might actually be the best thing that could have happened to you . . . and your closet.

27

A "SPECIAL DATE" MISTAKE

"Oh shit, THAT'S TODAY?!"

We've all done it. Forgotten a birthday, a holiday, an anniversary, or some other significant date in our relationship. Not only does it make you feel guilty, but it makes the other person feel, well, unimportant and underappreciated. But in the grand scheme of things, what does a day really matter? It's just a day, right?

True, every day is just another day. And, I agree, it wouldn't be that big of a deal if the previous 364 days were good ones because those memories and intentions will far outweigh whatever is happening (or was supposed to happen) today. Not to mention, given that the average person is going to live for, let's say, 27,393.8 days (or a little more than seventy-five years), missing a day or two doesn't seem like that big of deal.

Unfortunately, that is EXACTLY what makes it a big deal. It's the fact that it takes little to no effort to mark a day on your calendar that makes missing a particular day so inexcusable. When you forget little things, the other person is left thinking that you think little of them. *Make sense?*

Now, the problem with special dates and holidays is that we far too often use them as excuses to neglect each other until that day comes. We think to ourselves, *It's okay, I'll make it up to him/ her next month.* Then that month comes, and we do it again, and again, until we've neglected our partner for so long that an important day that is missed is more of a "straw that breaks the camel's back" than anything else.

So, my advice isn't to worry about the special days as much as you should worry about trying to make each day special. And it doesn't take much: a text, a note, an attentive conversation, a helping hand. If you show appreciation for one another, day in and day out, there won't be so much pressure placed on anniversaries, birthdays, Valentine's Day, etc.—these "special dates" will truly become just another day because every day is a day of appreciation. Now, I know it's not always easy to show up for each other every day—trust me, I speak from experience, as I have personally failed at this for months on end. Especially when you have children, work, and daily life on your mind, but I can promise you, it's doable. Although, it will take some getting used to. And, in the beginning, it might feel like work.

Lastly, remember, it's not *the day* that matters, it's *the time*. The other person wants to know that you are taking the time to acknowledge, appreciate, and respect them.

If you want someone to know that you *like* them, give them a gift. But if you want someone to know you that you *love* them, give them the gift of your time.

28

FOMO: FOCUS ON MOVING ON

In today's world, social media throws the "good times"—or at least the seemingly good times—in our faces more than ever before. And we all either contribute to, or succumb to, the online onslaught of hollow posting, humblebragging, and the never-ending stream of captions, videos, and photos all proclaiming, *Look what I'm doing!* We're guilty of viewing it, we're guilty of doing it, and we're guilty of feeling it whenever we're not the one doing it. So, if you're someone who derives your self-esteem from being seen, liked, or shared, the next few paragraphs are for you.

Now, whatever the reason for your feelings of envy, jealousy, or insignificance—not being invited to a big event, having prior commitments, or having an unhealthy addiction to viewing the lives of complete strangers that you have no real relationship with—the fear of missing out or, more simply, the feeling of missing out is, in my opinion, the leading cause of much of modern society's anxiety and depression. I'm fortunate enough to have grown up before social media turned the world upside down; I spent many weekends in high school and college doing absolutely nothing—without even a second's thought given to what I was potentially missing—and it was fucking awesome.

In today's clout-chasing digital landscape, with billions of people competing for relevance, far too many of us spend just as much, if not more, time focusing on the lives of others than we do focusing on our own. And, if you've ever tried to multitask two significant things at once, you've probably learned that it's not possible to get the best result from either one. And what's more significant than life itself? In other words, you cannot live your best life if you're constantly focusing on the lives of other people; your focus is scattered on shit that doesn't really matter. FOMO is a form of self-betrayal because it denies the importance of your own life. FOMO is a dildo that's quite literally fucking you into believing that your own life is boring. And, if you want to stop fucking yourself, you have to start focusing on yourself.

If you want to live your best life, you must redefine what FOMO means in your life. And, luckily for you, I titled this chapter with a suggested definition: Focus On Moving On. Focus on what's coming next in your own life. Focus on what you have ahead of you. Focus on whatever it is that you have to do—or can do— rather than dwelling on whatever it is that others are doing. Move on from the feeling of missing out and move forward with your own life—before you miss out on life itself.

29

YOU'VE BEEN "CANCELLED"

Whether you choose to spell it with one *l* or two, there's no denying that being cancelled can feel like absolute hell. Especially if it's your first rodeo.

Over the years, I've upset, annoyed, and downright offended thousands of people. And, well, some of these people have (on more than one occasion) suggested that I get cancelled. Unsuccessfully, of course. So, if you're being cancelled now, I'm going to tell you how to get this thing settled.

First, let's identify exactly why this is happening: Did you say something, do something, or suggest something that's actually wrong? Was it an honest mistake or did it come from a place of genuine hate? (Please note: If you did the latter and refuse to change your outlook on the matter, I can't help you. You're fucked and you might as well throw away this book because reading it with a closed mind is a waste of your time.) Now, if I had to guess, you probably made a mistake, told a joke that totally sucked, or said something a little too "fucked up" for popular opinion—none of which are situations that can't avoid cancellation.

Everybody fucks up. Everybody says or does things that they regret. Everybody needs to make mistakes in order to learn and develop into a better, stronger, more compassionate human being. Plain and simple, if we don't allow ourselves and others to fuck up, we don't allow anybody to grow up. And that's exactly how you need to view this situation. As frustrating as it might feel, you must treat this as an opportunity to grow; you will either learn something new or you will learn to stand for something that's meaningful to you.

Here are three ways to cancel being cancelled: 1) Take some time off, separate yourself from the noise of the internet, and focus on yourself. Let it blow over; it usually only takes seventy-two hours. 2) If you are truly remorseful for what you've done, own up to it. Sincerely apologize and move forward; let your actions do the speaking for a while. 3) If you have no regret for what you said or did—because it was and still is how you feel—don't apologize. Don't betray yourself for the sake of internet clout. Stick to your guns, and if you're considered a piece of shit for doing so, at least you'll be a piece of shit with integrity. Never stop being yourself just to please somebody else. There's quite literally nothing people respect more than somebody who stands their ground amid adversity, so long as the ground they stand on isn't built upon a foundation of hate and bigotry.

Trust me, everybody wishes they had the guts to ignore public criticism and keep going despite a mob of entitled morons attempting to cancel them. Hell, even those who want to see you fall yearn to have the courage to stand that tall.

30

WOKE UP ON THE WRONG SIDE OF THE BED

Occasionally, from the moment your eyes open in the morning, your day already seems to be heading in the wrong direction. Maybe you had a bad dream that left you with some unexplainable anxiety, maybe you had a bad night's sleep that has you easily annoyed and extra cranky, or perhaps, for no apparent reason—or at least not a reason that you can put your finger on—you just feel "off."

I find the "off" days to be some of the most difficult days to navigate because they don't seem to make any sense. At least if I know why I'm on edge, I know what thoughts to avoid in order to prevent my emotions from escalating. The problem with the days of mysterious agitation is that it feels like everything, and everyone, is the culprit and the reason why you feel like total fucking shit. On these days, nobody is immune to your bad mood, and nothing seems to work or go the way that it's supposed to: The coffee maker is too slow, the door requires you to push even though it says pull, and so on. Everything gets to you, and you just don't know why. Everyone around you is an annoyance, a disturbance, or a motherfucking problem. The good news: These feelings don't have to last all day. If you can get ahead of, well, your own head, you can still make the most of the day despite getting up on the wrong side of the bed.

When this happens to me, the solution that I've found to be the most beneficial (and reliable) is getting (and keeping) myself busy. The sooner, the better. It doesn't matter what it is—working, writing, physical activity, helping someone, etc., but whatever it is, it must be something that requires my full attention as I'm attempting to redirect my focus. It can't be something that I can multitask or something that I can half-ass while I continue to stew on everything that's bothering me. What I'm trying to do is simple: avert my attention so I'm forced to stop thinking about whatever the hell it is that has me feeling angry, annoyed, or hopeless. Think of it this way: The best way to kill a bad mood is to stop feeding it—you have to starve it of your attention and deny it your emotional reactions.

The less time that you allow yourself to dwell on feeling shitty for no apparent reason, the quicker you'll find yourself forgetting about those feelings altogether. The way I see it, bad moods are similar to bad relationships: You can't end things and move on until you stop giving attention to all the wrong things that have you holding on. And a proven way to stop giving your attention to someone or something that's negative is to refocus your attention on someone or something that's positive.

31

YOU'VE HIT A CREATIVE WALL

What's the difference between a creative block and procrastination?

In my opinion, nothing. I don't believe in creative blocks. I believe in low tide and high tide, but there is always something there—the well is never completely dry. Procrastination tells us we're empty, when in all actuality, we're just bored or lacking discipline. And if your creative waterline is currently low, here's what I believe will help you. . . .

Starting today, create a routine—a *ritual*, if you will—around your work. Write in the same room, adjust the lighting, turn off your phone, and play the same music (at least for the first thirty minutes or so). Do this every day, and every time, that you are ready to write, paint, play, draw, sculpt, or whatever else it is that defines your specific creative endeavor. After decades of creative work, I truly believe that you can train your mind to "turn on" by repeating the same ritual when it comes time to work. I have a specific set of songs that I play when I want to write, and I *only* use them to write. If one of these songs comes across a mix or radio station when I'm not writing, I skip it. My songs are reserved for creative work and creative work only. I want my brain to always associate them with creative time.

What I'm suggesting is an example of *classical conditioning*, also known as *Pavlovian conditioning*—your body and brain's response to external stimuli. A good example of this would be whenever a song comes on and you are immediately taken back to the same emotional state, even if only temporarily, that you were in when you first heard it *(c'mon, don't act like Linkin Park or Led Zeppelin doesn't do this for you)*. I believe you can do the same thing with your creativity, calling it back, by repeating a pattern of stimuli before you work, signaling to your brain that it's time to come online and create.

Now, like everything that's "work," some days will still be harder than others, and you will still need to take breaks, which are an equally important part of the creative process. And what I've found to be one of the best breaks from creative work is bodywork—in other words, exercise. Do something that allows you to turn off your creative brain and engage your body for a while: walk, run, lift weights, swim, have sex, etc. You NEED to step away from your creation from time to time in order to gain a new perspective. You can't manically work forever (unless you're using drugs) because there is a point of diminishing return in every creative session. Whenever you begin to blot the paint, repeat the same bars, make typos, or anything that makes the work worse than before, that is your signal to turn off the brain and engage the body before returning for another creative round.

Repeat this over and over, and you will eventually have a creation worth sharing. Then comes one of the hardest parts for any artist, musician, or writer: knowing when you are "done." For that, I'd like to share with you something that my father (a painter) once told me, *You're never done, you're just done with it.*

32

LOST LUGGAGE WHILE TRAVELING

This has never happened to me—but it is one of my greatest fears while flying. I'm more afraid of landing without my belongings than I am of the plane crashing. If the plane crashes, at least I know that I've lived a good life. But, if my bag is lost, I have to deal with airline customer service. And I'd honestly rather die than be placed on hold for that long.

Now, the reason losing a suitcase is such a significant incident is because, when we travel, we pack our best shit. We want to look good, feel good, and make the most of our vacation—so we bring the items that we believe will help us accomplish that. Consequently, losing your bag can literally feel like losing a part of your identity. Fortunately, I think I can help you regain some of it in the next few paragraphs.

If the airline drops the ball by dropping your bag in the wrong city, here's how I suggest you handle it: First, acknowledge that it sucks. It's okay to admit it as long as you don't dwell on it. Feel it, then deal with it. Because the sooner you handle it, the sooner you can start throwing back tequila shots. You still have an entire vacation to salvage. Hell, why settle for just salvaging it? Why not make it an experience that you'll never forget? In life, unexpected or unwanted situations can oftentimes lead to the best memories if we're simply willing to put aside the inconvenience and embrace the unknown or make the most of an unfortunate series of events.

So, unless you pack like a total fucking weirdo, you still have this book (obviously), your cellphone, and a credit card on you. And there are very few things in life or on vacation that can't be solved with this powerful combination. Of course, it's annoying to spend money that you hadn't planned on spending—but if a quick shopping spree for some clothes and bathroom necessities is enough to set you back considerably, you either have absurdly expensive tastes or you shouldn't even be on a vacation in the first place.

Treat this situation as an additional immersive experience in whatever city you're visiting. And, trust me, if you tell your story of loss to a few locals while you're shopping for essentials, they will readily provide you with recommendations to make the most of their city. If you can have a sense of humor about what happened, people will vibe off that energy. They will want to help you and/or live vicariously through you as they give you the rundown of all the best things to do in their town. Your trip won't be the one that you had planned, and you may never replace your favorite T-shirt (reread the chapter on ruining your favorite outfit for a refresher on that specific issue), but you'll absolutely have an experience worth talking about for years to come. Oh, and you can always extort the airline for some flight credit to use on your next vacation.

33

YOU'VE BEEN REJECTED

Rejection is often only thought of in terms of dating; however, rejection is something we face daily, especially if you're someone who's willing to try new things. And hopefully you're feeling the residual effects of rejection right now as you read this. I say "hopefully" because I'm proud of you for putting yourself out there.

Of course, rejection fucking hurts—that's why most people avoid it entirely—but nothing hurts as badly as never knowing, never trying, or never doing. That's a fact that many learn too late in life. It's the things left unsaid, the acts left undone, and the ideas left unrealized that will haunt you far more relentlessly than any form of rejection. So, again, if you've been rejected recently—GOOD FOR YOU—because it means you tried something new. Growth is the primary by-product of rejection, and each time you put yourself in a place of potential rejection, you're putting yourself in a place of guaranteed growth.

Maybe you shared an idea at work that was shot down by your boss, maybe you made a suggestion to your group of friends that wasn't taken seriously, or maybe you finally asked out that hot barista you see every morning only to receive a comment more bitter than the darkest of dark-ass coffee. Whatever it was, you're better because you did it. And every time you do it, rejection becomes increasingly less potent; you build up an immunity to it like you would to a poison. (Honestly, that barista isn't even that hot anyway; you just have a thing for them because you've associated their face with the best part of your day.)

As a writer, my ideas have been rejected hundreds of times. Had I taken each rejection as a sign to stop writing, I never would have written this book, which subsequently means you wouldn't be reading this. And hopefully by now this book has made you laugh, think, and ultimately feel better about things. My point is: Allowing rejection to prevent you from continuing, or trying again, can have repercussions that extend far beyond yourself and your temporary feelings.

We need people who are willing to be rejected in order for society to keep progressing. You never know when your willingness to keep going will create something that inspires or motivates others. Hell, even being rejected for a date might be something that made the other person's day. Imagine that individual just went through a painful breakup and the only reason they rejected you is because they simply weren't ready to date somebody new. But, because you were willing to shoot your shot, you flattered them, which gave them a boost of confidence that they carried into their next meeting, where they had the courage to speak up and share an idea that earned them a promotion. This might feel like a bit of a stretch, but it's not; serendipitous shit like this can, and does, happen— all because someone (possibly you) was willing to be rejected.

34

YOU'RE SICK AF

Maybe you've been looking forward to a party for months, maybe this big project at work could finally be your big break, or maybe you just can't wait to enjoy the weekend, but your body has other plans—because you're sick as a dog and twice as scraggly.

Now, before we go on, here's a quick history lesson about feeling like a dog: The origin of the phrase "sick as a dog" can be traced back to the 1700s when dogs were, sadly, linked to illnesses like the plague, which was widely spread by birds, rodents, and, yes, even man's best friend. (Huh, I guess you really do learn something new every day; I thought dogs only spread joy.)

Personally, there aren't many things that I despise more than being sick; I'm somewhat of a workaholic, so coming down with any affliction that's worthy of canine comparison tends to piss me off a bit. It's not so much the physical discomfort that gets to me as much as the mental toll of being unable to do what I want to do. For most of my life, I've disliked downtime; however, as I get older, getting sick has not only shown me the value of rest (I always recover more quickly when I do what's necessary to get over it), but being sick has also been an opportunity for me to practice setting and adhering to boundaries.

I know what you're probably thinking, *What the hell does getting sick have to do with boundaries, Captain?* Well, I'm about to tell you, and it has nothing to do with physical distance. It's safe to assume that most of us hate being sick (barring those who truly relish playing the role of the victim) because we don't like doing things when we already don't feel our best. Going to work, fulfilling your at-home obligations, studying for a test, etc.—all of these become considerably harder when we're under the weather. This is where boundaries come into play: Do you really have to deal with that today or can it wait? Are you willing to put yourself first for the sake of quickly recovering or are you going to drag out your symptoms because you don't have the courage to simply tell a person, *No, I'm not coming*?

Granted, there are legitimate times when taking a day off isn't a fucking option (parents know this to be the case all too well)—and I respect that; I once powered through salmonella because I had to be on a commercial set for two straight days—but most of the time, we're going to work, attending a friend's party, or putting ourselves in situations that make us feel worse because we're unwilling to put ourselves first. Being sick is the perfect time to practice saying *No* if you really don't want to go. Sick or not, far too many of us put ourselves on the back burner of life for the sake of what others might think if we choose otherwise.

At first, setting boundaries can feel overwhelming, especially when you're worried about what other people might be thinking (your boss, for example), but that's exactly why setting boundaries is so empowering— it's wild how much harmony can be found in a well-placed boundary.

35

WOKE UP WITH A HANGOVER

Holy shit—this is awesome. Do you remember saying that last night? Probably not. But one thing is for certain, you're not saying that this morning.

Now, most of this book has been focused on situations and occurrences that are, more or less, out of your control, things that just happen. As for the hangover, this is entirely your fault. However, that isn't to say that hangovers can't be just as surprising. I mean, you were having the night of your fucking life. And you probably even went to bed feeling pretty great (maybe a little horny or hungry, but great nonetheless). So, why do you feel so shitty today? You already know the answer to this, so I'm going to share with you my answer to dealing with it. Trust me, over the years, I've become a bit of a hangover aficionado.

When it comes to drinking, I try to abide by two rules. Rule Number 1: Drink a glass of water in between each glass of hard alcohol, or one water for every two beers. If I stick with this ratio, I can pretty much stay out all night—as long as there's a bathroom accessible. I might wake up feeling a little groggy, but it's nothing that I can't quickly shake off with exercise and some coffee (more on that later). Rule Number 2: Never drink for emotional reasons. Don't drink because you're angry, don't drink because you're worried, and definitely don't drink because you're heartbroken. Drinking for any of those reasons is a surefire way to have a terrible following day.

But what fun are rules when you're having fun? So, on the nights that you don't follow the above recommendations, here's a three-step process to curing a hangover—without drinking again; I know the "hair of the dog" feels good, but all it really does is prolong the recovery process. You need to hydrate, intake, and activate.

1) HYDRATE: You need to pound some water, preferably with electrolytes. 2) INTAKE: You need the three C's: caffeine, carbs, and cysteine. The stimulating effects of caffeine will help with your brain fog, the carbohydrates will help with your blood-sugar levels, and lastly, cysteine (something you've probably never even heard of) is an amino acid that helps your body produce the antioxidant glutathione, which becomes depleted in your body as you drink. And a great source of cysteine happens to be a delicious hangover cure: eggs. In other words, going out for a good breakfast the morning after drinking is both socially and scientifically the right move. 3) ACTIVATE: This one is the hardest, but that's why it's the most beneficial. Go for a walk. Hangovers, like most undesirable things in life, are made worse by sitting and sulking. Get outside and move.

BONUS TIP: If you're planning to drink heavily, order a steak for dinner (you know you want to anyway). Beef is rich in both vitamin B and zinc, both of which have been shown to reduce hangover symptoms. Now, *cheers!* And, you're welcome.

36

YOU'VE LOST YOUR SHIT

"Where did I put my keys?" "Where is my phone?" "Did somebody steal my wallet?"

The panic and frustration that comes from losing an important item is second to none. And the irony is that it's almost impossible to find whatever you're looking for if either of those emotions commandeer the search party; the more frustrated or fearful you get, the more you tend to forget. Looking for a lost item is a lot like arguing with a loved one: If you allow your emotions to take over, the situation is far from over. Sure, sometimes you get lucky, and your wallet miraculously appears in the middle of your meltdown, or the person you are arguing with suddenly understands your side of things—but most of the time, the longer it takes for you to cool off and think calmly, the longer it's going to take you to solve the problem efficiently. Nothing is going to help you find the phone that fell behind your bed more quickly than thinking with a level head. So, whenever you're looking for a lost item (for your sake, I hope you never lose this book), I suggest the first thing you do is calm down before you even begin to look.

I'm what many would consider an "on the surface" kind of human, meaning my emotions tend to live on the edge of constant expression. I'm not good at faking how I'm feeling, and I'm even worse at hiding my annoyances. This benefits me greatly with my writing and creativity, but when it comes to something like looking for a misplaced item, it's easy for me to lose focus and become visibly irritated.

However, something I've learned: If you actively engage in the act of calming yourself down whenever some annoying shit like this happens, you'll notice a profound change in your memory. You'll be able to recall names, stories, and the location of missing items much more effortlessly than before. Over the years, multiple psychological studies have shown that anger and memory loss are directly correlated. So, it would make sense that the less angry or frustrated you are, the better you'll be at recalling where you parked your car.

Seriously, take a minute to visit the comment section of any controversial social media post and witness just how many pissed-off folks can't hold an argument because they can't even remember what they're arguing about to begin with. In this case, it would seem the missing item that many of them are looking for is their goddamn mind. When we're angry, anxious, or aggravated, we operate at a level that's far below optimal. This is true in your relationships, this is true in your professional life, and this is especially true when you're crawling around on your hands and knees hunting for a set of lost keys. So, unless you want to look for them for fifteen minutes longer than necessary, calm down and allow yourself to think about the situation rationally before searching.

37

ONLINE ARGUMENTS AND ACCUSATIONS

In life, you'll be misunderstood. At some point, you'll be made out to be something you're not. When this happens, it's not as important to defend yourself as it is to know yourself. Know who you are, know what you mean, and know enough to feel secure even though you're not seen.

Online, every day, thousands of people fall to the mob of online trolls, overly sensitive individuals, and straight-up assholes. So, how should you respond when labels, assumptions, and misdirection are being used as a way to scare you into silencing yourself? Well, I'll tell you what I do because I'm no stranger to an online scandal.

Most people are too afraid to speak their mind—even if they believe it to be true—because they're overly concerned with how people will react to it, what they'll be called, or how their words will be misconstrued. At times, even I've found myself questioning what I say online (or write in this book) because of how my words might be appropriated or taken out of context. However, I'd rather live with the risk of being misinterpreted than the certainty of knowing that I was too afraid to say something. I'll go down with my ship if that's where my opinions and observations take me.

The access we have to information these days is mind-boggling. Our phones have turned most people's attention spans into a caffeinated cricket with nowhere to go, just bouncing from one place to the next with no purpose or conviction. That's good news for you. There's simply too much media, too many headlines, and too many polarizing distractions being thrown in everyone's faces these days for someone to stay targeted on you for more than a moment. If you remain confident in what you said or did—knowing your true intentions—all you really need to do is sit back and wait for people to get bored. I've learned to ignore online arguments and accusations the same way that a horse might ignore the flies on its face: I'm aware of their presence, but I'm also aware of the fact that they're harmless. The flies are there to feed on the horse's eye secretions, just like upset commenters are there to feed on the attention. Both represent a parasitic, pathetic relationship.

Online arguments remind me of siblings fighting over whose artwork will be displayed more prominently on the family fridge. Two adults going at it in the comment section of a post looks just like two children arguing for the attention and praise of their parents. The phrase "pick your battles" isn't just a platitudinal remark to justify standing down when you're not feeling it, it's quite literally one of the most effective bits of advice you could ever put into play regarding a social media tirade. Some battles aren't worth fighting, just like some flies aren't worth swatting. Lastly, go back and reread the opening paragraph of this chapter anytime you feel that your character is being questioned.

38

YOU'VE BEEN ROBBED

One spring afternoon in Los Angeles, I was walking to my truck in the parking garage where I lived at the time, only to see that the passenger door was wide open, and the interior had been completely ransacked. This was the first time that I'd been robbed. I'd never experienced anything like it before, and it felt pretty fucking violating. I immediately began tallying up my property losses, and the more the numbers added up, the more my rage boiled up.

After calculating just about two thousand dollars in stolen headphones, sunglasses, and a custom Bowie knife that was given to me as a gift, I called the police to file a report. Their response was, *This happens all the time; unless there's video evidence, there's nothing we can do.* Unfortunately, this made sense. I mean, what the fuck were they supposed to do? Issue an all-points bulletin to be on the lookout for somebody walking around with headphones, ladies' sunglasses, and a large knife? That doesn't exactly narrow down the search in an area like Venice Beach. So, I accepted the outcome, took the L, and got on with my day, completing the errands (sans sunglasses) that I had set out to run prior to learning what some asshole had done.

If I think back on this situation now, it doesn't bother me, not even in the slightest. The ordeal has served to make me more cautious about leaving items in my vehicle. And, honestly, it was one of the best lessons that I could have learned about the real value of material possessions. Although I liked those things, none of them were things that couldn't be replaced rather easily. I ended up buying cheaper sunglasses, cheaper headphones, and a pocketknife because the more expensive items didn't actually provide me with any more utility or joy than their more affordable counterparts.

Now, depending upon what was taken, your level of frustration will surely elevate. Hell, if my laptop were ever stolen, I'd lose my fucking mind for a time. But, even then, I know that with time I'd get over it because I have way too many other things to worry about than an object that I have little to no control over getting back. Somebody can steal your shit without your consent, but they can only steal your peace of mind if you allow it.

If you choose to look at your loss from a factual perspective—meaning how will the loss affect you in the grand scheme of life itself—you'll get over it much more quickly than if you choose to look at your loss from a personal perspective, which keeps you in a victim mind-set long after the incident. At that point, you're stealing from yourself: Prolonged victimhood robs you of the ability to feel good.

39

STUCK IN A RUT

When there's nothing particularly wrong with your life, but life still feels, well, *wrong*—what can you do? I mean, you have a good job, a decent home or apartment, a family, friends, and a loving dog (or at least a cat that acts very much like a dog)—and despite "having it all," you still feel "blah."

Unsurprisingly, this isn't a rare human feeling. I've felt it, your favorite celebrity has felt it, your ancestors felt it (but probably not as often because they were too busy farming and raising nineteen children), and now, you're feeling it. And while it's normal to occasionally feel stuck, it's not okay to allow yourself to remain stuck. Seriously, it's time to make a change. You're a human, a spiritual being, and a complex creature that needs to be challenged, excited, and actively engaged in your life in order to make the most of it. Just like animals kept in horrendous inner-city zoos require stimulation to prevent them from going crazy, you do too. We all need a purpose—without one, life becomes repetitive and tedious. Or worse, we, ourselves, begin to feel worthless. If you don't pull yourself out now, a rut can become a hole that traps you long-term.

Now, the hard part about a rut is that without a readily identifiable cause, it's confusing to fix. But, in all actuality, the fact that there is nothing particularly wrong means you have near endless possibilities to make it right; it could be something as simple as starting an exercise routine, or as dramatic as moving your entire family across country, or something in between. Ruts are actually great because they allow you to get creative, and creativity is a vital part of feeling fulfilled in life.

The first thing to realize about a rut is this: Your current life is a direct result of your past decisions, which may be difficult for some people to hear—but in order to accept the fact that you are capable of changing your life moving forward, you have to also accept the fact that you are responsible for your life thus far.

If you're not ready to hear this, your natural response will be to get defensive: *But I didn't choose for this to happen, I was the victim, it wasn't my fault....* And, yes, that might be true. But what are YOU doing about it now? If you remain stuck in what has happened to you in the past, you will ALWAYS feel stuck in the present, which means your future will never move forward. Until you find purpose in your past, you'll continue to find excuses in the present, and you'll always feel like a victim of life—instead of someone with life experience.

If you don't know where to begin, start with something small, and work up from there. Change your morning routine, pursue something artistic that you've been avoiding, find a new hobby, read some books—and if that's not enough, move on to the larger stuff: new job, new city, new relationship, or perhaps a new face *(I'm kidding, you don't need plastic surgery—but, then again, I don't know you personally)*. Whatever you do, do it for you. After all, it's YOUR rut, and only you can pull yourself out and no longer be stagnant—relying on someone else to pull out might just get you pregnant, which can create a whole different scenario if you're not ready for it.

40

FELL FOR A FINANCIAL SCAM

Maybe you failed to do your research, maybe the person on the other end was just damn good at what they do, or maybe the outcome just seemed too good for you to turn away. However you were scammed, understand that this shit happens, often. Even some of the most brilliant financial minds were fooled by Bernie Madoff, as he made off with billions before anyone was wise to him. All I'm saying is, if a bunch of wealthy investors and Ivy League–educated banker bros can be fooled, there's no reason why it can't happen to you. Bummer, I know, but all you can really do now is look at the facts: How did this happen? Where did it go wrong? What are the warning signs to look for in the future?

And equally as important as reviewing how it happened is how you choose to treat yourself now that is has happened. Whether it's a pump-and-dump stock scheme, a crypto that you purchased based on a meme, a get-rich-quick pitch by some poser on Instagram, or a "loan" given to an ex-lover, beating yourself up over it is not going to get your money back.

Here's the deal: According to a data book published in 2021 by the Federal Trade Commission, 44 percent of fraud reports involving a loss of money came from individuals twenty to twenty-nine years of age.* Forty-four percent. That's a hell of a lot of scamming happening to young, supposedly "I'm too intelligent for it to happen to me" individuals. For comparison, the same data book revealed that only 20 percent of financial fraud reports came from individuals seventy to seventy-nine years of age. Now, keep in mind, these numbers are just loose estimates of total fraud because they're taken from the people who actually reported being taken advantage of—the real numbers are likely much higher because nobody wants to admit to getting scammed out of their hard-earned money. So, if you've been scammed, you're not gullible—you're human. Stop feeling stupid, don't let your humiliation prevent you from seeing a good opportunity in the future, and don't allow this to impede you from taking a risk that could both personally and financially be totally fucking worth it. Calculated risks are what make life worth living. On the contrary, too-good-to-be-true risks can make life feel unbearable. Do your homework. Ask questions. Don't make monetary decisions based on emotion.

And be more forgiving of yourself and more empathetic toward others. Unless the person asking for your compassion is a foreign prince requesting your credit card information via email or direct message—that fucking dude is definitely trying to scam you.

---

* Consumer Sentinel Network Data Book 2020: https://www.ftc.gov/system /files/documents/reports/consumer-sentinel-network-data-book-2020 /csn_annual_data_book_2020.pdf, Executive Summary, page 5

41

BITTEN BY A RATTLESNAKE

One minute you're hiking, trying to take the perfect picture for Instagram so everybody knows you're "outdoorsy"—the next minute, you're quite literally fighting for your life due to a rattlesnake bite. You know, the snake whose picture was posted on all those "Danger: Watch for Rattlesnakes" signs at the trailhead. The upside: If your crush doesn't like the picture that you posted right before being bitten, at least the snake thought you looked like a snack. Anyway, I'm an Eagle Scout, so let me help you figure this out.

First, you should call for help immediately. If you have cell service, use your phone for something other than attempting to impress people and dial 9–1–1. Be sure to note the exact time that the bite occurred because you'll need to track the progress of swelling in addition to the time remaining for the optimal effectiveness of antivenom.

Now, say you don't have the reception needed to get ahold of a professional: First of all, good for you for hiking somewhere that's actually in the wilderness; although, it would be a lot more convenient to be near a busy street right now. Control your breathing, heart rate, and anxiety as much as possible. Panic will only increase blood flow, which will cause the toxins to spread more rapidly. Do whatever you can to get to an area to receive help by moving as little as possible. If someone can carry you, great. If you're on your own, try to immobilize the area to the best of your ability. In this moment, a calm, cool, and collected demeanor can literally save your life. And, oddly enough, that same demeanor can work wonders in your dating life—keep that in mind after you survive this thing. And, finally, remove any restrictive clothing from the area to allow for swelling. (There's definitely another joke to make here, but this is a life-or-death situation, so let's get on with it.)

Well, if you've made it this far into reading about your rattlesnake bite, you really need to stop reading this book and get your ass to a hospital—one that treats snake bites, not heartbreak. A hospital that treats heartbreak is called a bar and that's the last place you need to be right now because alcohol thins your blood and that will most certainly make your snake bite a hell of a lot worse. Believe me, I love beer as much as anyone (probably more), but no beer or amount of social media clout is worth dying over.

42

REGRET PARTING WAYS

Oh, NOW you want it. An object, a job, or a relationship. We've all done this: let something go, only to later realize that we should have held on to it. And that unexpected regret can hit like a ton of nonreturnable bricks. "You don't know what you've got till it's gone" isn't a phrase that's been passed down from one generation to the next for no apparent reason. It's been passed down because it couldn't be more accurate. Now, I can't directly help you get something or someone back—there are far too many nuances to be taken into consideration for any specific advice to be given—but what I can do is help you come to terms with it. And, more importantly, stop the incessant craving to look back on it.

Throughout my own life, I've dealt with the regret of letting something slip more times than I care to admit. I'm a ruminator, and I love to reminisce on situations and scenarios, thinking of how I'd do things differently now. For me, I feel as though this thought process is both a gift and a curse because reliving past experiences is what fuels a lot of my work (most of this book came to be because of this very behavior). I intentionally replay situations in my head until I find a unique, meaningful, or teachable perspective that I believe others will relate to; unfortunately, this means it's all too easy for me to spend too much time overthinking my decisions. So, when it comes to wanting something back, I can surely empathize with your sentiment.

I also know that wishing for something that's already gone is a thought process that's completely counterproductive and progressively destructive. In recent years, I don't do it nearly as much as I used to, and I'm a hell of a lot happier, successful, and well off because of it. All areas of my life have benefited from separating myself from those thoughts. Criticizing yourself for walking away from a relationship, quitting a job, or giving something up is never going to bring it back. In fact, it's likely going to prevent you from ever receiving something equally as meaningful, if not more so, in future scenarios. If you gave something up, the best thing you can do now is focus on leveling up—without it.

Get to work, get other aspects of your life together, and get over the feeling that you've "fucked up." When you do this, you'll be surprised by how quickly you not only forget, but also how quickly you find happiness in other shit. And maybe, just maybe, don't bank on it—this outlook, and a purposeful existence, just might be what brings whatever it is that you were missing in the first place back into your life someday. The universe has a funny way of testing us like that.

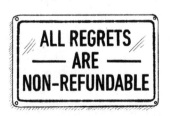

43

YOU'VE LET YOURSELF GO

Honestly, this shouldn't be much of a surprise; these kinds of things happen with time. What can be surprising, however, is how quickly time flies. One day, you might just wake up and realize that you're not happy with where you are, who you are, or what you're doing. Now what?

Whether it's physical, financial, or mental, nobody likes feeling like they've let themselves go. Perhaps you've become too complacent at a job, too comfortable in a relationship, or too addicted to the same routine and way of doing things. All of these are valid reasons to feel upset, especially when life seems to be ticking away—fortunately, these are all capable of being corrected.

The term "letting yourself go" is most synonymous with our physical appearance, but it's a term that everyone should consciously apply to their relationships, personal life, career, mental health, and spirituality. Far too many individuals are walking around blinded to their own complacency. If anything in your life has gotten heavy, complacency is what created that weight. As you're reading this, if you are currently feeling this way about one of the areas that I just mentioned above, you're ahead of the game; most people never catch it. Or worse, they catch it, but never do anything about it. So, now that you know you've let yourself go, how are you going to turn your shit around and stop letting yourself down?

Here's what has worked for me. . . .

The key to getting any piece of your life back on track—or perhaps on a track that it's never been on before—is not finding the motivation to do so; it's developing the discipline that will make it happen. Discipline is the glue to not only make sure your to-dos actually get done, but it's also a way to cultivate the accountability to hold yourself to 'em. In simpler glue terms, self-discipline makes you stick to shit. When the right choices become habits, you can pull yourself out of pretty much any rut. You can recover a sinking career, you can strengthen a broken relationship, and you can completely change your physical appearance. So, make a plan to get unstuck. Then, make a promise to yourself that you will do anything necessary to not fuck it up. Don't just promise yourself that you'll do your best— promise yourself that you'll do it until you get your desired results. Engage in change with the intention and determination to reach your chosen destination with no other option.

When you make the conscious decision to see your life through resolute vision, you'll see what's coming and you won't ever be surprised again by that sudden "I've let myself go" feeling.

44

LEAKED NUDES OR A SEX TAPE

Be pissed, be upset, be sad. Be whatever the hell it is you want to be now that everybody has seen, well, everything. But, don't allow yourself to believe that it's the end of everything. Either you're giving the power of your nudes too much credit or you're giving the situation too much of your attention.

Your privacy has been violated—and you have every right to feel wronged—because that video or those pics weren't meant to be seen by everyone (if it makes you feel better, I didn't look). And, although they were shared without your permission, the situation, oddly enough, now requires your permission to keep going (to an extent). Here's what I mean by that statement: The less of a reaction that you give the situation, the sooner the situation will be over. That's just how human nature, scandals, and society's tech-driven attention span work. Essentially, if you decide you want to address it briefly, make a joke about it, or act like it never happened, that's up to you—but whatever it is that you choose to do, do one and be done with it. Treat the situation like a bad one-night stand: Give it your attention for a moment, then never again. There's always the option of pursuing legal recourse as well, but as I've mentioned before, I'm not a lawyer. So, you'll need to talk to somebody else about that.

Have you ever noticed how quickly certain celebrities, powerful politicians, or high-profile CEOs are able to move on from shocking personal news? Well, not only do these individuals hire the best of the best when it comes to publicists, but the masterful move that many of them employ is to change the subject to something new. When you do this, the audience either falls for the distraction or loses interest altogether—because your reaction doesn't play to their voyeurism. It's sickening, really, how much enjoyment people get by prying into somebody else's private shit.

To your advantage, people nowadays are bombarded by so much scandalous behavior that they simply have no desire to pay attention to one naked person forever. It's only the situations or individuals that continue providing updates that keep online conversations ablaze. So, if you want to put out the fire started by your hotness, stop giving it fuel; either give people something else to focus on or just let your bare body burn out over time. Now, I know it's hard to not give every second of your waking attention to something that feels so violating. But, as the saying goes, life truly is 10 percent what happens to you and 90 percent how you react. Everything, and I mean everything, can be overcome. Everything can make you a better person in the long run. Even a bunch of strangers seeing you naked can make you a more confident person.

Not to mention, if you're not shy, and you really want to turn a negative into a positive, perhaps you can use a bunch of strangers seeing your private parts as a fresh start—a lot of celebrities have used leaked nudes as the jump start their careers needed. If the scandal doesn't go away, you might just have a new career opportunity.

45

CREDIT FRAUD

From blowing out your candles to stealing the punchline of your joke, what motivates somebody else to steal the credit or the attention that's due for, well, somebody else? Although we don't know exactly what motivates them in each situation, it's more than likely rooted in jealousy, envy, low self-esteem, or an egotism that simply makes them believe they can get away with it (because they have before). At work, a colleague might take credit for your idea; at home, a sibling might take credit for doing a chore; at the bar, a friend might take credit for your clever pick-up line—credit fraud like this happens every day, in a variety of ways. And it's fucking annoying. So, how do you react when it happens to you?

Chances are, you react a lot like me: First, you pause for a moment and think to yourself, *What the fuck? Did that really just happen?* Then, after mental confirmation, you have an immediate desire to get even—but is it actually worth it? Should you call them out in front of a crowd? Should you wait for an opportunity to deliver a low blow later in the night? Should you pull them aside and have a private conversation? Depending upon the circumstance, and my relationship with the individual, I could go with any one of these options, or a combination.

However, there's another way to handle the matter. And it's the route that's most often chosen by masters. Those who are leaders, creators, and true originators actually take it as a compliment, and a challenge to continue creating things that are worth stealing. I get it, hearing the phrase *Imitation is the sincerest form of flattery* used to infuriate me. I hated the idea that I should be flattered by somebody else's flat-out plagiarism. Then, after seeing my writing misappropriated thousands of times over the years—I realized that if I didn't start learning to deal with these occurrences in a productive way, I was going to continue allowing something that was completely out of my control to hijack my mood, my creativity, and my individuality.

Here's a fact about life: Anything noteworthy, anything humorous, and anything worth a damn will be copied, misused, and stolen by those who lack the ability to think, create, or do it themselves. You can't stop this; it's as likely to happen as the sun is to rise each morning. But, what separates you from them is the ability to do it again, and again, and again. Put it this way: They can take something, but they cannot take where that something came from. So, do your thing. Create your way. Be your authentic, funny-as-fuck self. Rewards are found in repetition and frauds are eventually revealed. At the end of each day, take pride in the fact that—no matter how many people try to be you—YOU are the only one who will actually be you. And that's something that can never be taken from you.

GET YOUR OWN IDEAS

12/21

THE CAPTAIN

46

OUTNUMBERED OR UNSUPPORTED

Maybe your family doesn't support your business goals, maybe your friends don't understand your creative flow, or maybe your wife/husband just doesn't "get you" like you wish they would. There's a lot of reasons why we feel alone or unsupported—but there are even more reasons why you can still succeed without the support of others. Now, I'm not suggesting that you turn your back and abandon those closest to you—but, if it comes down to doing it alone or not doing it at all, by all means, do it alone if you have to.

The honest truth: You don't need people to believe in you if you believe in yourself. Of course it's easier, more fun, and even more rewarding to have a team working toward a common goal, but if you want something bad enough, you—and you alone—can find a way to make your dreams a reality. And the first step toward making that happen is removing the belief that you are owed anything. Your friends don't owe you their support, your spouse doesn't owe you their unwavering belief (even the healthiest of relationships have boundaries), and the world certainly doesn't owe you anything. If you are someone who can't make things happen for yourself, without feeling unlucky or left out, then you are going to have a hard time accomplishing anything. There is truthfully no more effective killer of dreams than a victimhood mentality.

Here's the deal: No matter how great your idea, not everybody is going to get it—but that doesn't mean you should forget it (or forget them). Not having someone's support is vastly different from outright sabotage. If those close to you are sabotaging your dreams, well, you probably need to drop them from your life. But if they just don't seem to get what you're doing, or don't share the same vision or aggression to make something happen, you just need to do it without 'em. The beauty of feeling like it's you against the world is that you get to decide who to let into your world now, or later when you make your dreams a reality.

And remember, in the game of chess, even a lonely pawn can become the most powerful piece on the board; all it has to do is successfully move to the last rank of the other side. Likewise, you can become something (or somebody) more than you are today; all you have to do is continue making moves and moving forward—*with or without the support of those around you.*

47

SORRY, WRONG PERSON

Oh shit, now they know how you truly feel about them. That text wasn't meant for them, it was meant to be *about* them.

That's a good thing, right? I mean, isn't honesty easier than pretending? No? Not right now? Well, then take the mistake as a wake-up call to stop gossiping—or, if you're going to gossip, don't say anything about someone that you wouldn't be okay with them reading in a text accidentally sent directly to them. Because, at some point, it's going to happen.

You'll be surprised at how much easier your life becomes when you make the conscious decision to be honest with everyone—especially yourself. I wish I had adopted this mind-set earlier in my life; it would have saved me so much time, spared me a lot of drama, and prevented the misplacing of much-needed energy. If something isn't working, if you and a person just aren't vibing, or if a friendship isn't one that you see yourself in for long, admit that to yourself, to them, and move on. Isn't that far more productive than gossiping about them and the situation for years on end?

When you stop gossiping or engulfing yourself in the drama of others, you change the energy that you project, multiply, and attract. You become a magnet for meaningful interactions instead of a lure for hollow humans. However, this can only happen to its full extent when we're honest with ourselves about who or what we truly want in our life. And, once you've filled your life with people who fulfill you, and vice versa, you'll never run the risk of this type of texting situation happening again because you'll be at a place in your life where gossiping isn't something that you ever feel the need to engage in or propagate. Gossiping is fucking pointless when your life has purpose. Some of you might be nodding your head while reading that last line because you, yourself, used to be a drama-loving individual, and now you know just how much peace a gossip-free existence can bring. It's a great fucking thing, and the people in it are even better.

DISCLAIMER: It's worth noting the possibility that a missent text was actually something positive. Perhaps you sent a text admitting you have a crush on someone. But, you sent it directly to the crush in question because your brain turns to mush whenever you think about them. If this is the case, don't be embarrassed—own it. This way you can either stop wasting your time or start realizing your desires. Both are clearly wins. Better yet, don't even wait for a texting mistake to happen. If you like someone, just fucking tell them. Because playing it cool all the time is a great way to ensure that you'll be playing with yourself most of the time.

Sorry, wrong person.

48

TRIGGERED

One minute you were just having fun, or so you thought; the next minute, someone is having a motherfucking meltdown. Maybe it was a game, a joke (probably a good one), or some advice that seemed harmless, but now the other person is about ready to cut your throat over something that wasn't really that serious. Hell, maybe you're the "other person" in this scenario and something has triggered you.

Now, we've all experienced this type of situation before. And, the majority of the time, your instincts are correct: What was said wasn't that serious. However, when something playful or light-hearted hits on something personal or guarded, the tides of good times can abruptly swell to a sea of seething anger, defensive behavior, or deep melancholy. Why is that? Well, it's because our past experiences, going as far back as our early childhood years, can, and will, influence our reactions to comments and situations for the rest of our lives—IF we leave issues unresolved or undiscovered entirely.

When a comment "strikes a nerve," it quite literally strikes a nerve. Our memories are stored as neuronal connections within our brains, and when one of these connections is tapped—whether consciously or subconsciously—we're triggered to react. This is why it can take mere seconds for a moment to go from playful to painful.

For example: When a joke hits on a personal insecurity, it's hard to not react defensively because it reminds us of a time when we felt stupid, unloved, or wrong. Whether we remember exactly when and why, well, therein lies the mystery and opportunity; whatever triggers us, teaches us. And, if we make ourselves aware of these triggers, we can start the process of recognizing what larger issues might be lying beneath the surface. To put it another way, triggers are like the tabs on the side of a binder: They can help us quickly find things that we've filed away.

When others appear to take something too seriously, or when we do so ourselves, it's almost always reflective of a past experience and not the particular moment. In life, we are going to say things that will trigger others in ways that we didn't intend, and vice versa. Now, this will happen to some of us more than others. Hell, spend five minutes on any social media network and you'll see more triggered folks than there are words in this book. However, triggers are an invitation to remove whatever anchor is attached to them. Keep this in mind as you traverse through life. Then, the next time you upset someone with a joke, or somebody totally roasts you with one of their own, you might not feel so bad about it. Or, at the very least, you can learn from it.

49

KINK IN YOUR NECK

Nothing reveals your age quite like a random neck injury. As a kid, you could literally sleep like a crumpled-up marionette doll carelessly tossed in a box and still wake up feeling like a million bucks. But, once you hit a certain age, all it takes is spending more than twenty minutes sleeping in the wrong direction and you'll wake up feeling like Dr. Frankenstein's monstrous creation—stiff, confused, and cranky as hell. In fact, I have a kink in my neck as I write this, and I absolutely feel like a creature that's been bolted together.

I can't turn my head to drive properly, I can't have a conversation without looking like I'm flinching in pain over something that was just said, and I most likely won't be going to the gym (RIP my new routine). Anyway, I thought it was oddly appropriate that something as seemingly insignificant as a stiff neck muscle has been enough to affect so many aspects of my day because, well, the entire premise of this book is to find ways to avoid having unexpected things like this do just that.

So, with that in mind, I decided to turn my day around by utilizing my neck pain as inspiration to write this chapter. Not only to help me forget about it, but also because I know we've all dealt with it. And, just like that, even the most ridiculously miniscule annoyance now has a purpose. As a writer, finding purpose in the negative, the uncomfortable, and the undesirable has helped me handle the majority of life's adversities. Now, unless you're also a writer, you probably won't find the same inspiration from all conditions; but that doesn't mean you can't ask yourself the same question that I do whenever I find myself in an unfavorable situation: *How do I give this meaning?* If you ask yourself this scrupulous question each time you're hit with something undesirable, you can't help but think about the ordeal differently—most likely, in a way that helps you more easily deal with it. Maybe you plan to use it as a teaching moment for your kids, an experience to connect more closely with a friend, or a story to tell at your next AA meeting. Shared experiences connect us to humanity (even something as ludicrous as a sleep-related neck injury). And sometimes the purpose of going through something is simply to remind you of the fact that you're human.

Until then, alternate between hot and cold compresses, and promise yourself that you'll never take a day free of neck pain for granted again. Afterall, every day that you don't wake up feeling (or looking) like Frankenstein's monster is a gift. The little things in life truly do matter; it just sucks that it can take something as annoying as a kink in your neck to serve as that reminder.

50

BAMBOOZLED BY SOMEBODY

Have you ever met somebody only to soon find out that pretty much everything you thought you knew about them was wrong? Now, I'm obviously not talking about the times when somebody pleasantly surprises us; I'm referring to the times when somebody completely fools us. Like a magician pulling a rabbit from a hat, they've managed to pull the wool over your eyes, leaving you feeling as though you bought tickets to a show instead of engaging with a real individual.

Maybe it was somebody you were dating, maybe it was a friend that you thought had a stronger character, or maybe it was an employer that promised you one thing only to end up doing another. Whatever the situation or person, seeing somebody's true colors for the first time can be truly disappointing— particularly when we've invested our time, our energy, or even a piece of our life into an expected outcome: a serious relationship, a heartfelt friendship, or a promising career.

As humans, it's not always easy to not place a part of ourselves into those we believe in, but when we do this, we set ourselves up to feel like something's missing if the situation turns out to be something other than we imagined. This is especially true during the times that we find ourselves in a particularly vulnerable emotional position. Immediately following a breakup, during a time of prolonged unemployment, or perhaps a period of deep loneliness and isolation are just a few of life's many scenarios that make us extra vulnerable to deception by a group or an individual. When we're searching for something, it's easy to try to find the answer in somebody.

Sure, your desperation, good nature, or tolerant demeanor may have been taken advantage of, but you can still use this situation to your advantage. Nothing in life will help you build more trust in yourself than realizing that you truly are the only person you, without question, can put your trust in. That's not meant to sound cynical; it's beneficial and rewarding to trust others, but none of that matters if you can't trust yourself first and foremost. And what better way to develop trust in yourself than to be alone with yourself? Trust me, I know it sounds shitty, but no other moments in my life have helped me build more self-confidence, self-respect, and self-reliance than moments when I've been forced to realize that I'd put too much trust in others, and not enough trust in myself. And, sometimes, we need a harsh reminder, or an unexpected letdown, to rebalance the scale of trust in our favor. . . . Also, remember to always trust your gut whenever shit isn't adding up. It doesn't take a mathematician to know when 2 + 2 = somebody fucking with you.

51

SO, YOU'RE GOING TO BE A DAD

Now, I'm writing this from a man's (my) point of view because I'm clearly not in a position to speak from a woman's perspective on this. There are too many variables that go into getting pregnant and staying pregnant, and your decisions are your decisions. I'm not even about to attempt to make suggestions about something that I can never personally experience. However, I am a dad, and I do believe there's something in the following paragraphs that will benefit any expecting parent—particularly those who weren't expecting it.

At the time that I'm writing this, my son is four months old. And he is undoubtedly the best thing that has ever happened to me. That's not just some cliché for the sake of saying something cliché—I actually fucking hate clichés—but I can think of no better way to express the grandiosity of his influence on my life in just four short months. That statement is a staggering realization that I didn't anticipate having when I first heard the words *I'm pregnant.*

When I came home to my then-girlfriend, aka "the enchanted mother-to-be," brandishing a plastic stick covered in her pee like an object of sorcery, the results couldn't have been more unexpected to me (although they should have been expected because my pull-out game is weak as shit). As the weeks went on, and I began to absorb the magnitude of becoming a father, I had a difficult time not absorbing the hopelessness of the "your life is over" commentary that I received from other men, some women, and a lot of complete strangers. Simply put, I wasn't ready to become a dad; I thought I had about ten childless years left in my coffer. So, the doubt that these comments planted in my mind began to work overtime. Then, one day, I snapped out of it when I finally opened my eyes to the obvious fact that those projecting their pessimism onto my impending fatherhood were/are individuals whose lives (many of them parents themselves) I would never want to emulate. Their unfulfilling lives had nothing to do with having kids and everything to do with them and their own lack of initiative. I realized that becoming a dad—like nearly any significant life change—was going to be whatever I wanted it to be. And, when the fog of fatherhood fear finally cleared, my concerns turned to excitement. I was excited for the new journey, the new perspective, and the new life that was coming, not only into my world, and his soon-to-be-mom's world, but into the entire world.

Here's the deal: Far too many individuals use their kids as a convenient excuse for their inconveniences. Furthermore, they view having children as the primary reason their life didn't become what they had envisioned it would. Not only is this belief ludicrously mistaken and unfair to your children, it's a pathetic way for any person to view their life. Being a father has given me a purpose, perspective, and pleasure that has actually made me more creative and ambitious than ever. So, if you're about to become a dad, congratulations. It's going to be so fucking awesome.

52

WHEN COURT IS YOUR ONLY OPTION

Take it from me, you don't want to go to court, arbitration, or any other form of legal negotiation. It all sucks. I don't care how good your lawyer is—even if your lawyer is your dad—the legal process is an absolute pain in the ass and "legalese" is written to make you feel dumb, wrong, and insecure. I literally don't wish legal trouble on anyone—except maybe my worst enemy because fuck 'em—but as for you, I feel for you if you're going through it. I've been there, it's no fun, and I'm sorry you're dealing with it. There's literally no such thing as an easy or enjoyable legal battle.

In fact, the very root of the word "legal" tells you that it's going to suck. "Legal" comes from the Latin word "le," which means "to," and the Greek word "gal," which means "suck" (a connotation referring to old-world Greco-Roman prostitution), and there you have it:

Legal = To Suck . . . okay, I totally just made all that shit up. "Legal" comes from the Latin word "legalis," which is a derivative of the word "lex," meaning "law." But I think my definition is more accurate, and hopefully it made you laugh because there won't be much laughter during the remainder of your legal proceedings.

Now, it's normal for anything legal to stress you out and make you feel incompetent; the legal system relies on you overreacting, worrying, and feeling unprepared because you will need to hire an expert to help you. Legal paperwork is intentionally written to be difficult for the everyday individual to decipher and defend without a lawyer. It's a racket, but if you find yourself with no other options but to sue someone, well then, you're going to have to get into bed with a lawyer. Not literally. *(I mean, unless you can pay off your legal bills that way— then you might want to consider it because legal bills are fucking expensive.)*

Having dealt with the legal system myself, here's what I recommend.

1. HIRE A PRO: Trust me, without legal experience, you can really fuck things up for yourself, but a *good* lawyer will save money, time, and even some of your sanity. Let your lawyer do their job.

2. STAY BUSY: Do whatever you can to <u>not</u> think about your legal trouble. Once you've filed and done everything on your end, forget about it as much as possible.

3. SETTLE IN FOR THE LONG HAUL: Even the best case can drag on forever. And, honestly, opposing lawyers will drag things out just to increase their own billable hours. So, don't expect it to be over quickly. Plan on it taking forever, and you'll be happy when it's over within a year or two.

4. LEARN FROM IT: How can you prevent this from happening again? What decisions (if any) did you make that contributed to this situation? Personally, I've become very shrewd with my business relationships because of this. If it doesn't feel right for any reason, I don't do it—even if there's an opportunity—simply because I don't want to go through any legal shit again. It's just not worth the headache.

Other than that, I wish you the best. Sorry it has come to this, but you gotta do what you gotta do—and, sometimes, the only way to let people know that they can't fuck with you is to take 'em to court.

53

MISSED YOUR SHOT

You were prepared. The opportunity was there. And you wanted it more than ever. So, what the fuck happened? You had it in the bag.

Whether it's a metaphorical miss, or a literal air ball over the basket, we miss shots all the time. Bombing a big presentation, missing the goal that would have won the game, or completely blanking out while trying to get the right words out—it happens. And it's going to happen again. Right? I mean, it better happen again. Because missing your shot is no reason to miss out on the chance to miss again.

The billionaire entrepreneur Richard Branson once said, *Opportunities are like buses, there's always another one coming.* So, unless you insist on only taking Ubers (you bougie bitch), this quote applies to each and every one of us. You may have missed this opportunity, but if you put yourself back in the proper position—either in life or in a game—there will be many more opportunities for you. Maybe there's something that you can learn from this round and apply to the next round (like the superior Blackjack card counter that I referenced earlier in this book), or maybe shit just happens and your desired outcome wasn't meant to happen for you this time around. Either way, every miss is an experience, and every experience will prepare you for the next one. Not to mention, misses build character. And character creates far more winners than talent alone. Fundamentally, the more character that you build from missing, the more you increase your likelihood of winning.

For that reason, I'd much rather have a life full of misses than a life with only one or two memorable wins. All those misses are going to become relatable stories, and all those stories can become motivation for others while simultaneously serving as moments of profound reflection for yourself. Think about it this way: Would you rather have a conversation with somebody who won the high school championship and quit playing after that, or somebody who lost that game but still went on to play professionally? You'd obviously choose the latter individual— the individual who has missed far more than the individual who quit after high school. Let's be honest, this entire book would be utter shit if all I did was tell you about all the times that I got life right, while leaving out each time that I missed, messed up, or mishandled a situation along the way.

If we don't miss, we can't truly appreciate the win. So, keep missing, and when it comes time for celebrating, be sure to reminisce on every miss that it took to get there.

54

YOU'RE LATE

Ugh, not again . . . First things first, if you're in traffic right now, seeking some advice on dealing with your road rage, put this book down and focus on the road, please. If that's not the case, feel free to continue reading and let's talk about your tidsoptimistic tendencies.

Now I don't know about you, but whenever I know I'm going to be late, I get anxious, my palms get sweaty (it's hard to not place some Eminem lyrics here), and everything frustrates me. I hate being late. Maybe it's because of the way that I was raised, maybe it's because I take my word seriously when I say *I'll be there,* or maybe it's just an anal part of my personality that I need to overcome. And, since I don't see the latter becoming true any time soon—I sincerely believe timeliness is a significant sign of respect for others—here's a weird mental method that I use whenever I know I'm about to be late to something that I've committed to, which might work for you too. First, let whoever is waiting on you know that you're running behind, because there's nothing more selfish than being a no-call, no-show type of individual. Then, tell yourself that time is now out of your control because, well, it is. And, although you've lost the battle with the clock, what remains within your control is how you choose to show up.

What's worse than showing up late? Showing up late and angry, and stressed, and as an all-around fucking mess. I'm typically opposed to saying this, or propagating the idea of faking anything, but alleviating your mind of the negativity that comes from running behind is quite literally a "fake it 'til you make it" scenario; fake being in a decent mood until you make it to your destination (or do whatever you can to actually get yourself into that mood for real). If you do this, the energy that you bring into the room when you finally do arrive will make you a welcome atmospheric addition, which makes waiting around for you feel more than worth it.

The majority of people will be forgiving of you being late if you: 1) Let them know you're going to be late and 2) show up in a good mood (looking good helps too). If you've ever waited for someone to join a meeting, or you work in a client-centric industry, I'm sure you've felt this before: When somebody finally shows up—and they show up in a bad fucking mood— you generally wish they'd never shown up at all. So, if you're already going to be late, what else do you have to lose, except the bad mood?

Also, relax. Being late happens, but when it becomes a habit, you have a problem. And, if this is your problem, you don't need a new watch; you need an interpersonal intervention about respecting your fellow human beings and their time.

55

STEPPED IN DOG SHIT

"What the fuck is that smell?"

You check your area, you check your breath (you might want to reevaluate who you've been kissing), and lastly, you check your shoes . . . yep, you just stepped in dog shit. And, to make matters worse, you've tracked it onto the carpet. Now what? Easy, you clean that shit up—because you're an adult and you know how to handle a shitty situation. Done and done, let's move on. But, what about the figurative dog shit that we step in far too often in our everyday lives?

Throughout each day, we both knowingly and accidentally often step in metaphorical dog shit. Dog shit like gossip-filled conversations, dog shit like arguments that are simply not worth having, and dog shit in the form of bad energy picked up from a particular person or situation. And, unlike its canine counterpart, this kind of dog shit is not always as easy to clean up. Emotional dog shit is stickier, heavier, and harder to remove because, with or without shoes, it clings to you. And you'll drag it with you—brushing it onto others—for the rest of your day, week, or longer.

Now, going back to real dog shit for a moment, our greatest worry about stepping in it is tracking it into our car, the office, or our apartment. Just one small misstep can quite literally get shit everywhere. This is true with emotional dog shit as well. Emotional dog shit needs to be avoided with the same level of care because once you've stepped into that conversation, spent time browsing that person's Instagram, or allowed somebody's fecal vibes to rub off on you, you're going to carry that shit with you for a while before you realize what has happened. And that shitty feeling can rub off on all areas of your life: your work, your downtime, your relationships, etc.

So, how can you avoid emotional dog shit, the type of dog shit that you can't exactly see or smell? Well, it's tricky, but you do so by paying attention to how things make you feel. I'm not saying avoid anything that makes you feel bad, because a lot of good can come from facing negative emotions. I'm talking about avoiding the conversations, the situations, and the persons that clearly leave you feeling shitty—minus the personal growth opportunity. When you've stepped in emotional dog shit, you'll know it. Because you'll feel it. It's empty, it's depressing, and it stinks. And, if you do choose to keep stepping in it, you'll eventually become the dog shit that others are trying to avoid dealing with.

56

A SORE LOSER AND A SORE THUMB

"1–2–3–4 . . ."—do you really care whether or not you win a thumb war?

C'mon, you can't be THAT competitive. Sure, friendly rivalry is fun, but it's even better when you can lose, laugh, and move on.

Don't get me wrong, competition is great; in fact, I think it's necessary in many aspects of society—and I personally hate to lose—but when competition becomes an obsession and your self-worth is based solely upon winning, well, you're going to go through much of life feeling like a fucking loser. Not to mention, you're going to miss out on a lot of personal growth, character development, and opportunity.

Because the truth is, losing is one of the most—if not THE most—effective ways to succeed. Don't believe me? Ask anyone who has reached a high level of success what taught them more: Winning or losing? And I guarantee you that at least 95 percent of them will say losing (the remaining 5 percent are liars trying to maintain an image by refusing to admit how many times they've actually lost).

You learn better by losing because it's undesirable—yes, even something as stupid as a thumb war can teach you things, like character and not taking life so seriously. If you're a sore loser, you're definitely a sore thumb to yourself and others. Nobody wants to be around someone who can't lose and move on from on it. You want to really know what separates winners from losers? *Losers lose and stay there—winners lose and move on.*

Now, if you can't remove the competitive spirit from everything you do, it's most likely because deep down, you have an insecurity of not being enough. If you're on top, you see yourself as on the bottom. And it's this kind of black-or-white thinking that keeps losers down, unable to see the nuances of life and the fact that you can lose and still not be a loser. You are not your wins, nor your losses, you are a human who either wins or loses: Of course, winning is enjoyable, but at what cost? Is it worth your sanity to turn everything into a competition? Nobody wants to hang out with that person.

 Besides, not all loss is a loss; sometimes, you need a loss to become a fucking boss. Begin by losing the parts of your lifestyle that no longer serve you, lose the behaviors in your life that no longer represent you, and definitely lose whatever attitude has you believing the world owes you. You only owe it to yourself to not base your entire self-worth on winning every little thing.

57

GOT AN STD (MAYBE?)

In this scenario, what's more surprising, the itching or the burning?

Hopefully, there's not also a third surprise, *Who the hell gave this to me?* You might know, you might not; it all depends on your lifestyle. And I'm not here to tell you to put your pants on. (I mean, definitely keep them on until you figure this thing out though.)

Now, let me tell you a story . . . back in, well, you don't need to know the exact year, I had my own STD scare. And I was fucking stressed. The worst part about it was feeling "dirty," like I was tainted and nobody in their right mind would ever want to be intimate with me again. So, if you're reading this and are currently going through your own *Oh shit, I think I caught something!* moment, I know your fears. And guess what? If it turns out that you do have something, your fears are accurate to an extent. I'm not going to lie to you. People are freaked the fuck out by STDs, and rightfully so.

However, STDs are not the death sentence of your sex life that society has conditioned us to believe. A temporary halt? Sure. But a coitus coffin? Probably not. Granted, different STDs carry with them varying levels of severity and treatment. Some are curable, some only manageable. In your scenario, only time will tell. Regardless, you must know. So, if you think you may have caught a case of crotch crickets, make an appointment and get your shit checked out.

Fortunately for me, my run-in was just my imagination run amuck (looking back, it's a funny story). All tests revealed that I was totally fine—but I'll never forget the way that I felt about myself during that time. I had never experienced that level of shame and regret before. For twenty-four hours, I legitimately hated myself, which is a feeling that I'd wish upon no one—no matter the situation, no matter the condition, no matter the disease, disorder, or diagnosis.

The gist: Either you treat it, or you learn to live with it. Listen to your doctor, and life will go on. What has happened does not make you any less of a human. It does not make you dirty, tainted, or broken. It doesn't mean you're doomed to be alone. You're still the same person you were before this, and in most cases, with treatment, you'll be fine in a few weeks.

58

SOMEBODY ATE YOUR LEFTOVERS

"Hey, I was saving that!"

You clearly put it in there to eat later. You couldn't have written your name any bigger. You even took the time to hide the container in the back of the refrigerator (you know, behind that old jar of pickles that's been sitting in there for what seems like forever). However, despite taking every precaution, your leftovers have been eaten by some other person—what a dick move.

Whether this happens at work, at home, or anywhere else you've chosen to stash your leftover Chicken Parmesan, somebody eating your leftovers feels a lot like somebody kissing you without permission: Neither flavor was theirs to savor. So, what do you do now? Do you say something? Do you eat somebody else's food, thus starting a chain reaction of illicit food consumption? Do you order from a delivery app and just pretend it never happened? Two of those are clearly trick questions because there's really only one appropriate choice in this situation. The behaviors that you allow from other people become their habits—and if their habits negatively affect you, you had better speak up so that bullshit doesn't continue.

For some, having your leftovers eaten might not be substantial enough to justify a confrontation; for others, it's an act of war. I happen to side with the latter because it's blatantly disrespectful to take something that obviously isn't yours. It could be a friend, a family member, a partner, or a co-worker—whoever it is—if they knowingly take something from you without your permission, they are basically stating, *I deserve this more than you do.* They're brazenly ranking themselves above you on both the metaphorical and the figurative food chain. And, if you don't stick up for yourself, that ranking will continue to take precedence in their life and yours. Although eating leftovers might seem miniscule, it's not so inconsequential when you consider what the act is communicating in regard to hierarchical status.

I'm not saying you need to go rushing into their room or office like a warrior ready to destroy an enemy's fortress, but you should embody that same type of courage any time you need to let somebody know that how they've treated you is not okay. It may be the way a family member talks to you in front of your friends (or anyone, for that matter), the disregard a partner has for your feelings, or the continued lack of respect shown

by an employer. If you don't acknowledge your disapproval by standing up for yourself, you are inaudibly giving them permission to do it again.

Now, if the leftover larceny continues to happen after

you've talked with them, I strongly suggest you resort to teaching them a lesson. Try leaving something in the fridge that looks absolutely fucking delicious, but pack it full of laxatives. Then, remove the toilet paper from all the bathrooms so they know exactly what it feels like to not have something waiting for them when they want it.

59

WHEN YOU GOTTA GO, YOU GOTTA . . .

In an effort to stay regular, I thought I'd take this as an opportunity to transition seamlessly from the last line of the previous chapter.

It starts with a bubble, a bit of a cramp, and then a full-on panic attack. When your stomach catches you off guard, your entire body sounds the alarm. You become a survivalist of sorts: scanning the room for viable exits, counting just how many steps it will take for you to get there, perhaps even debating whether or not it's worth waiting. Trust me, it's not; just handle it—in public.

Now, I know this might seem like a rather mundane matter to some of you, but you'd be surprised to know just how many people have an extreme aversion and fear of public bathrooms.

As an adult, there's nothing more embarrassing than shitting your pants, except maybe crying on national television because you were voted off a silly dating show (where you believed you were in love with a person who you only knew for one episode). When nature calls at the worst possible time—in a meeting, on an airplane, or while sitting across from somebody extremely attractive—don't let your pride fool you into believing you can "just hold it." In this moment, every minute is precious, and every minute that you waste trying to act like you're not in pain is a minute that you literally inch closer to ruining your favorite pair of underwear. Hey, shit happens, and nobody is immune to undercooked food, a stomach flu, or half a bottle of hot sauce; there's no shame in excusing yourself before you lose yourself.

Here's a shitty story for you: I was once headed to the airport for a long flight across the country—Las Vegas to Miami; prior to this, I had way too much coffee. Let's just say my stomach was experiencing turbulence before I even arrived at the terminal. After thirty minutes of fighting the inevitable while simultaneously fighting mid-afternoon traffic, I drove my rental car over a concrete median, and ran into the closest convenience store, only to find that the bathroom was out of order. Now, really nervous and somewhat sweaty, I quickly scanned the parking lot and slipped through the back door of an adjacent bakery. Behind an "Employees Only" sign, I found what I desperately needed to find.

The moral of the story: I thought I could sort things out when I got to the airport, but that was a mistake that I will never make again. The longer I waited, the closer I came to spoiling my entire day. And there's a lesson here that goes beyond bowel movements: At some point in all our lives, we will feel as though we're being summoned to do something. Maybe it's taking a new job, moving to a new country, or making a complete one-eighty in the way you're living—the longer we ignore these feelings, the more painful life will become. All I'm saying is, when nature calls, answer it. And, when life beckons, act on it.

60

BFF BACKSTABBING

There aren't many things in life that take us back as unexpectedly as finding out that somebody—whom we genuinely believed had our back—has chosen to stab us in the back instead. Unfortunately, backstabbing isn't something reserved solely for rulers of ancient Rome or movie scenes depicting medieval power struggles. Backstabbing happens often, and the results can leave us feeling dumb, devastated, and disheartened. Afterall, not all friends are who we thought they were; moreover, even the best of friends, and the sincerest of individuals, can make a mistake. But, that doesn't change the fact that backstabbing is a conscious decision that one must make. This is why backstabbing is difficult to reconcile. Once we feel betrayed, it's hard to feel safe.

Now, I can think of a few standout occasions when I've been backstabbed by a friend, but I cannot think of a single occasion when that same friend did it to me again. Why? Because we either worked things out by coming to a mutual understanding with a level of forgiveness that carried our friendship through any future situation, or I simply cut that person out of my life forever. If your friendship is strong enough to work it out, with both persons comprehending what exactly happened and why, you'll be better friends because of it. But, if the other person remains unashamed, then that person is not your friend. Maybe they were at one point in your life, but they certainly aren't now. And cutting them out of your life is most likely the only way to make it right.

Losing a friend is hard, but not as hard as feeling the need to constantly overexplain yourself, protect your interests, or look over your shoulder because somebody can't be trusted. The loss of a heartfelt friendship feels similar to a legitimate death. It's the mourning of a connection that is no more, but I assure you, doing this is going to help you move forward. Because life is too short to live with the worry that you'll be backstabbed by a so-called friend. Life is too precious to waste it with people that are malicious as opposed to loyal. Simply put, life is hard enough already; you don't need the added concern of being stabbed—figuratively, or in Julius Caesar's case, literally.

Not to mention, sometimes true friends come back around after they've had time to reflect, grow, and realize the error of their ways. But that will never happen if you don't leave them to figure it out on their own in the first place. You can't wait around for someone to get their shit together, especially after they've already hurt you with their behavior. In an ideal world, backstabbing would never happen—but because humans are far from utopian beings, you occasionally have to turn your back and walk away if you want to live your life, in your best way.

61

JUST CAN'T CATCH A BREAK

Now, maybe this entire book has been a harsh reminder of all that's currently going wrong in your life. And, unfortunately, life doesn't take breaks to allow us to catch our breath. Fate won't hold back while we adjust our footing. Time can't be paused so we can brace ourselves for what's coming. Life just hits. And, when it hits, all you can do at times is take it. But that doesn't mean you have to allow it to take you down. You're not a victim of circumstance unless you allow yourself to be one.

Sure, there's a good chance that life really is working you over right now. Maybe life is indeed hitting you with the ol' one-two punch more often than ever before—I've been there—but as long as you keep fighting, you're doing exactly what you need to do in order to set yourself up for that "break" you're looking for. Catching a break is a lot like catching a wave: You have to actively paddle if you want the wave to take you. (I don't even surf and I know that.)

Here's the thing: Shitty shit happens. Sometimes, in rapid succession. It happens to you, it happens to me, and it has definitely happened to anyone you've chosen to idolize or envy for whatever reason. Occasionally, these hits come so hard and fast that simply getting up in the morning feels like facing the ten-count of a title fight. And, every time we feel overwhelmed by too much, or too little, it's imperative that we look back on all the times that we've felt this way before. To have come as far as you already have in life, you've had to overcome a barrage of life's punches, and you'll do it again. Circumstances that you thought would be the end of you actually ended up making you. Look back on every time in your life that you were going through something that you felt you wouldn't survive: a devastating heartbreak, the death of a pet, the loss of a job, a life-threatening injury, etc. If you're alive (which you must be if you're reading this), you've pulled yourself through some shit that felt impossible at the time. Replay those successes and use them as affirmations that you're capable of getting through this situation.

In other words, if you're frustrated and depressed by a variety of things in life that are "just not going right," that doesn't mean it's time to hang up your gloves and call it good. If anything, it might just mean it's time to fight dirty. Now, I'm not suggesting that you start breaking some laws and shit, but if you're truly feeling suffocated by life, it's time to start rethinking how you're going about things. And, well, sometimes you have to get dirty before you can get clean. Meaning, the muck that you're currently dwelling in might just be the test you need to prove to yourself that you're capable of handling anything.

Lastly, to wrap this up as an easy-to-remember one-liner: When nothing in life seems to be going your way, all you can do is, well, keep going. . . .

62

ABDUCTED BY ALIENS

Okay, so the unexplainable happened: You've been abducted by aliens and (unfortunately) returned to Earth—with a story that nobody will believe . . . or so you think.

Well, shit, how do you deal with something like this? Do you tell someone and run the risk of being labeled the "crazy abductee" for the rest of your life? Because you know that everything you ever say from that point on will be met with the snide response, *Yeah, but weren't you also abducted by aliens?* That doesn't sound fun. Except, the only other option is to keep the experience to yourself, allowing it to slowly eat away at your sanity, your self-esteem, and your view of the world around you. Which, to me, sounds a hell of a lot worse than being labeled crazy. I'd much rather be called "crazy" by others than to believe it about myself.

So, if I were ever taken to outer space on a field trip without a signed permission slip, I'd definitely tell somebody about it. I'd just be very selective about sharing my experience as an extraterrestrial's science experiment. I'd tell a trusted partner, a confidant, someone I know is just as open-minded as they are down-to-earth. Also, someone who knows me well enough to know that I wouldn't just make shit up. When something indescribable happens to us, talking about it can be just as disturbing as the event itself, which is why it's important we share with someone who gets us. Conversely, if somebody has chosen to share their experience with you, it means they've selected you as that person—don't take that lightly.

Now, here's the unfortunate truth about life: Damaging shit will happen to us that other people will not believe (or choose not to believe). I'm just using alien abduction as one example because, ever since I was a kid, it's always been my worst nightmare (*Fire in the Sky* really fucked me up). And, although we won't all be subjected to the same struggles and situations, there will always be one thing that we all have in common: our ability to help each other recover and move forward. When we talk, and allow others to talk, we connect over our shared humanity, which creates the space to heal. At first, it might take a while for you to build up the courage and comfort to tell even a single individual about what happened to you, let alone a group, but it's a far better struggle to endure than a lifetime of suppression.

When bad shit happens, when dreadful memories weigh us down, when doubt tells us that nobody will believe what we're talking about—that's exactly when we need to talk about it the most. It is through talking that we not only find the words to move forward for ourselves, but we also enable others to find a similar strength within themselves.

63

DISASTROUS DATING

I get it, dating can be frustrating. Trust me, those two words rhyme for a reason—similar to the alliteration of the words "hungry" and "horny"—because dating is basically the same as grocery shopping: You know what you should be looking for, but all bets are off when you see something delicious and bad for you. . . . And, with social media, apps, politics, and a world of increasing polarization, it might be harder than ever to find someone you get along with, let alone somebody with whom you can envision spending your life with.

Now, as easy as it is to blame a shallow, gator-infested dating pool for all of your repeated dating woes, the truth is: It's probably you. As much as you may not want to hear it—particularly when you're sad, tired, and alone—who you attract into your life is often a direct reflection of who you are. I know the cliché is that "opposites attract," but that's only true with magnets and one-night stands. Anything long-lasting is going to require common beliefs, similar energy, and a shared direction. That's not to say that there can't be exceptions when it comes to the complexity of human attraction—but if the overwhelming majority of your dates, relationships, or "situationships" seem to be ending the same way, then it's definitely you. When a pattern repeats, and you're the common element in that chain, you have to take that for what it is: a wake-up call.

This DOES NOT mean you're a bad person, or an undesirable, "undateable" individual; it simply means you have a pattern that you need to recognize when it comes to how you date and who you date. And, once you realize what might be creating these recurring scenarios, you'll feel more positive and powerful than ever. You will have more control of your life, and more importantly, who you allow into it.

Because your life works like an algorithm: The more attention you give something, the more it appears in your life. Consider this when constantly telling yourself that *everybody sucks, dating is awful,* and *all men/women are the same.* Trust me, if that's what you believe, that is what you will continue to receive.

The beauty of the above statement is that you can become the sort of person who you hope to attract. With that in mind, you should approach dating with the idea of leading with your whole self, showing people who you really are early on to make sure you align. Because when you know exactly what it is that you bring to the table, and also what you would like the person sitting across from you to bring to the table, you'll be able to set the table correctly to develop a connection that lasts well beyond the first course.

64

BUGGED BEFORE BEDTIME

Picture this: Just as you're crawling into bed . . . you see something crawling across the wall. What do you do: Do you ignore it because you've had a long day? Do you freak out and run from the room? Do you turn on the light and kill whatever the hell it is? There's a multitude of ways to handle an unwelcome houseguest, but which reaction is best?

Well, if it's a cockroach, I'll crush that little fucker faster than a frat boy can crush a beer can. If it's a spider, I'll probably leave it. (Unless it's something that I know to be lethal; if that's the case, I'm sending that eight-legged death demon back to hell before it can send me to the hospital.) However, if the exoskeleton in question scurries away before I can identify it, I'm probably going to spend too much of my night thinking about it, which is honestly the worst outcome of all. Because not only do I still have an unidentified creature in my bedroom, but my sleep schedule is going to be fucked by thinking about it.

Because it's not often what's actually there that keeps us awake at night—a spider, for example—it's the thoughts that we weave about that spider that give us anxiety (I mean, unless the spider is playing a tiny violin just to be annoying). Similarly, the thoughts about a meeting, an upsetting social interaction, or an exceptionally bad day can leave us feeling as though we're stuck in a web of stress. Or, as the title of this chapter would suggest, we're simply too bugged to go to bed. And, yes, I know a spider is an arachnid and technically not a bug.

Anyway, this all-too-common situation can teach us a valuable lesson about our thoughts. If our thoughts can so easily keep us up at night, then they can just as easily keep us in the fight. Throughout this book, I've discussed an abundance of awkward scenarios, undesirable situations, and unfortunate occurrences that have the potential to completely ruin our days, our weeks, or even our lives. And, however random each circumstance might have been selected, they share a commonality for successfully overcoming them: how we choose to think about them. Like a spider, your mind can entwine you in thoughts of stress, fear, and hopelessness. Or your mind can spin a web of ideas to escape, resolve, and brave whatever it is that has you feeling helpless.

So, the next time you see a spider in your room, or something unfortunate happens to you—before you allow your mind to race, do your best to squash that shit in its place (or remove it if you're not into killing). Remember who you are, revisit a few of these chapters if necessary, and rest easy knowing that you got this.

65

YOUR BOAT HAS A HOLE IN IT

I'll be honest, I don't know shit about fixing a hole in a hull, but I do know a lot about the importance of setting goals. And a boat with a hole is a lot like a life without any goals: They both share the feeling of sinking.

For me, I'm happiest when I'm working on something that gives me purpose, day in and day out. For example, I made it a goal to work on this book for at least two hours every day until it was finished. Doing so kept me focused and forced me to make constant progress, regardless of whatever else was happening in my life. If I missed a day of writing, I felt like I let myself down. If I missed two consecutive days, I started to feel as though I was drowning because it meant that I had an increasing amount of catching up to do.

It might not have been noticeably apparent throughout this book, but like many of you, I'm prone to bouts of depression and negative thinking. In fact, that's exactly why I wanted to write this book in the first place. As someone who can easily "go there" when it comes to getting down, I believed I could offer some valuable insights as to how I've prevented myself from spiraling in a variety of situations. And having goals to constantly work toward has been paramount to keeping me afloat at times when it has felt like life was trying to take me under. If I'm not working toward something, I feel like I'm sinking. However, when I am actively pursuing a new objective, I feel rather unsinkable.

It is true that the invention of the boat changed the world. It made new forms of commerce, travel, discovery, and war all possible. Up until the invention of the airplane, boats represented the ultimate form of freedom and potential (in many areas, they still do). But that potential can only be realized if the hull of the boat is in optimal condition. With a solid hull, a boat can withstand storms, attacks, unexpected encounters with the Kraken, and whatever other crazy shit life throws at her. Likewise, I believe a driven, purposeful existence will do the same for any individual. A life with goals will keep you focused, and optimistic, despite the waves of turmoil that will undoubtedly crash around you from time to time. Your goals will become the hull that keeps your life afloat. Your goals will allow you to live your life in a state of intention instead of a state of constant reaction.

Now, I chose to end the book with this story and metaphor because, with these last few words, I will have effectively completed my goal (until I start the next book, of course). All in all, I hope this book helped you laugh, helped you heal, and, most importantly, helped you see the potential to overcome everything and keep on sailing. . . .

ABOUT THE AUTHOR

Writer. Creator. Instigator.

Dad, but not your dad.

The Captain